Spiritual Integrity

Spiritual Integrity

On the Possibility of Steadfast Honesty in Faith and Worship

Martin S. Cohen

Hamilton Books
Lanham • Boulder • New York • Toronto • London

Published by Hamilton Books
An imprint of The Rowman & Littlefield Publishing Group, Inc.
4501 Forbes Boulevard, Suite 200, Lanham, Maryland 20706
Hamilton Books Acquisitions Department (301) 459-3366

6 Tinworth Street, London SE11 5AL, United Kingdom

Copyright © 2021 by The Rowman & Littlefield Publishing Group, Inc.

All rights reserved. No part of this book may be produced in any form or by any electronic means, including information storage and retrieval systems, without written permission from the publisher, except by a reviewer who may quote passages in a review.

British Library Cataloguing in Publication Information Available

Library of Congress Control Number: 2020915074

ISBN: 978-0-7618-7239-9 (pbk.)
ISBN: 978-0-7618-7240-5 (electronic)

Contents

Preface	vii
1 The First Gate: Knowing God	1
2 The Second Gate: Believing in God	23
3 The Third Gate: Reading God	35
4 The Fourth Gate: Praying to God	55
5 The Fifth Gate: Worshiping God	63
6 The Sixth Gate: Obeying God	89
7 The Seventh Gate: Standing before God	105
8 The Eighth Gate: Living with God in the World	117
9 The Ninth Gate: Loving God	131
10 The Tenth Gate: Cleaving unto God	137
Afterword	161
List of Abbreviations	163
Index	165

Preface

If your religious education was like most people's, it consisted of someone—a man or a woman, a teacher or a clergyperson, a dedicated professional or a well-meaning amateur—telling you things that would have sounded to you as delusional fantasies in almost any other context. When you were still young enough, and naïve enough, to ask obvious questions—and also, perhaps, before you were old enough fully to have understood that Andersen's story, "The Emperor's New Clothes," was meant as a cautionary tale for adults and not solely as a celebration of children's candor—you may well have asked some of the obvious questions that the lessons you were being taught would naturally have prompted. How did your teacher know the Bible is true? How, if God is beyond the ken of human beings, did your teacher seem nevertheless to know so much about the workings of the divine realm and the will of heaven? If every faith preserves a canon of sacred books it claims reveal the will of God—and if each of those faiths presents its adherents with a different set of ritual and dogmatic requirements—then must not embracing one of them imply the tacit rejection of the others as, to say the very least, spurious and misconceived?

If you asked those questions once, you probably didn't ask them a second time. On the other hand, if you *did* ask them, and if you had a charitable, good-hearted teacher used to the openness and guilelessness of children, then it was probably explained to you that your questions weren't so much unanswerable as unaskable, that your questions themselves—rooted as they were in your assumption that things either are or aren't true—made no sense in the context of the study of religion. It would have been explained to you that there is such a thing as spiritual or religious truth that is distinct from—and in some ways wholly unlike—scientific truth. You would have been given to understand, either gently or harshly, that such questions simply *cannot* be asked because matters of faith—in this wholly unlike a scientist's untested hypotheses—are simply not open for negotiation or, even more absurdly, experimentation.

The word "faith" would probably have come up a lot if you were the kind of student who asked sharp, incisive questions. Existing, somehow, at the confluence of knowledge and hope, faith was—and, in many circles, still is—deemed a profound enough concept to solve all these problems by declaring them invalid in the first place, hence unworthy of being debated or even discussed at too great length. You were probably told that you would understand later on what adults mean by this great catch-all concept and how it can be used to make religion not only meaningful, but profoundly so, even in the absence of empirically provable, scientifically demonstrable, and logically reasonable data. Furthermore, you were probably made to feel that the problems you were raising were basically your own, not ones rooted in the system of religious faith and action in which you were being instructed. If your experience was anything like mine, you were possibly also made to feel not only foolish for having asked too many unanswerable questions, but also just a little base for having impugned with your childish insolence the basis of the very religion your parents were doling out all that money for someone to teach you all about and to inspire you personally to embrace.

You were right the first time. Faith—at least when the word is used to mean belief in something there is no specific way to verify—*is* the refuge of scoundrels, a mighty fortress of dogma and doctrine built on the kind of ever-shifting sand that can only support such an elaborate edifice briefly, if at all. There *is* no such thing as knowing something you have no way of learning . . . or of possessing information you have never actually acquired. Declaring openly, even fervently, that you believe something to be true when you have no specific way to know whether what you are asserting is fantasy or reality, is not merely folly, but, if it involves lying about God, it is blasphemy as well. In the end, the path to truth cannot, logically *or* practically, be paved with lies, not really even *some* of the time and no matter how convenient it would be—and, believe me, it would be *very* convenient—if such were not to be the case.

As a rabbi and a Jew, I have written this book *about* Judaism. But the basic principles that underlie every one of its chapters—that claiming to know what cannot be known is lying, that no amount of pious insistence can magically alter reality, that the search for God can never be successfully undertaken (let alone successfully concluded) other than in an atmosphere of absolute, unwavering honesty, and that there is no valid distinction whatsoever to be made between religious and scientific truth—these principles can be applied with equally unsettling effect to all religions and systems of human spirituality. I mostly write in Jewish terms because I find it natural to express myself in the language I speak best. But I don't think that the issues relating to spiritual integrity I wish to raise here are *specifically* Jewish issues. Just the opposite is the case, in fact: it is the willingness to embrace, not this or that specific article of dogma, but the larger concept of conducting their spiritual lives in a context of unyielding, uncompromising and unwavering spiritual integrity that links the honest faithful of all religious groups to each other and makes it reasonable to think of them all as children of the God whose succor they seek and to whose service they wish to devote themselves. And it is also what separates them, at least emotionally, from the fanatics and fundamentalists of their own religious groups, men and women whose spiritual lives are dedicated to precisely the opposite principle: that someone with a loud enough voice can make a statement true by repeating it often and fervently enough, and by impugning the spiritual *bona fides* of any who dare demur.

At its base, Judaism is a collection of underlying principles and articles of faith that have been made both accessible and embraceable through the process of ritualization. There is no real question that the process works well enough to give perceptible, physical presence to the dogmatic beliefs of Judaism in the everyday lives of actual people, but that process has a negative side as well. Indeed, for all the system as it has evolved wrests the principles of faith from the hands of disinterested idea-mongers and makes of them the generative energy source at the center of Jewish life as it is actually lived, it *also* submerges those same principles under a blanket of rules and technical procedures that make them difficult to discern at times even for people totally devoted to their faith. Yes, you can ignore the issue and rely on the fact that these fundamental principles exist at the core of Jewish life whether or not they are formally acknowledged. (In other words, you can make your peace with ignoring them and rely on the fact that they surely *must* exist even if left unidentified and unacknowledged, not at all unlike the way it feels reasonable to suppose that the girders and beams that support a building also *must* exist—and crucially so with respect to the people inside the structure—whether or not they are visible to the naked eye.) Nonetheless, declining to identify these principles is intentionally to disable your ability to grapple with them, thus reducing to nil the possibility of real spiritual growth through their agency. And choosing to esteem adherence to ritual as an end unto itself is also wrong because, at least in my opinion, the great challenge that faces every successive generation of Jewish people is *precisely* the task of identifying afresh these core beliefs . . . and, in so doing, becoming able to decide rationally and thoughtfully which of them should be retained as part of that generation's effort to use the core beliefs of their own ancestors to create a highway that can lead them toward intimacy and communion with God.

There are those in the world who fear this kind of quasi-archeological interest in what lies beneath the surface of religious life because they sense, entirely correctly, that it may well lead to untraditional conclusions regarding their own religious beliefs or practices. I have rejected that kind of thinking mostly because it is unappealingly suffused with pessimism and the dread of despair, but also because it reflects a lack of faith in the intellectual capacity of normal people to evaluate their beliefs and to use them in a sensitive and intelligent way—and in an atmosphere of absolute spiritual integrity—to pave a path forward that they themselves can then follow. To put it differently, I have come to believe that the goal of religion is to enable men and women who yearn for God actually to walk with God, as Scripture has it, and thus to cleave unto the divine Presence without leaning on crutches of intellectual feebleness or on the perceived obligation to limit the power of the unrestrained imagination to think mindfully and honestly about God. Indeed, it is only from the starting point of unrestrained readiness to free the imagination from any preconceived rules and obligations that can ever come the ability to embrace the kind of intellectual freedom that I have come to consider the highway to communion with God, whom tradition aptly describes both as the Freedom of the world *and* as its Will.

Forcing myself to isolate these ideas and then to weave them into a single theological statement that represents, even inadequately, what I have learned from a lifetime of teaching and preaching has been a bracing undertaking and a humbling one. Whether I have succeeded in creating a way for modern men and women to embrace religion without feeling some sort of concomitant obligation to disable their own intellectual integrity is for others to say. All I myself can say is that I have done my best.

Citations from the Mishnah's tractate Avot, popularly called Pirkei Avot, follow *Pirkei Avot Lev Shalem,* edited by myself and featuring commentaries by Tamar Elad-Appelbaum and Gordon Tucker, which was published by the Rabbinical Assembly in 2018.

The image on the cover of this book, derived from the Hebrew text of Psalm 85:12, was taken from Rabbi Menasseh ben Israel's self-published *De Creatione Problemata XXX* (Amsterdam, 1635) and also appeared in his *De Resurrectione Mortuorum* (1636), as well as in his editions of Aisik Tyrnan's *Minhagim* (1636) and Solomon ibn Verga's *Shevet Yehudah* (1638). The Hebrew words *emet mei-eretz titzmaḥ* mean "From the earth shall truth sprout forth."

Astute readers with backgrounds in Hebrew will note that I have translated verses from the Bible here and there just a bit idiosyncratically, preferencing (as I always do) what I hear over what I see. Nor have I made any effort to distinguish between the various names of God that appear in the Hebrew text, feeling that such distinctions would be somewhere between distracting and undecipherable for most readers. As a result, I have used the English "God" for several different divine names and have occasionally used "the Eternal, your God" when the context required a double divine epithet.

Preface

I have tried out the ideas set forward in this book in many different contexts and settings over the years and I would like to thank all my colleagues who have read and responded to parts of this manuscript in the course of the almost two decades that I have been working on it. Also, and especially, I would like to thank the leadership and membership of the congregation I serve, the Shelter Rock Jewish Center in Roslyn, New York, all of whom have been endlessly supportive of my writing and who clearly understand that that my writing is part of my service to them . . . and, through them, to the larger world of people who care deeply about religion in general and about Judaism in particular. I am grateful to them all, and particularly for the thoughtful, interesting feedback I received after early versions of material from several chapters of this book were published in *Siddur Tzur Yisrael*, the two-volume prayer book published by Shelter Rock almost fifteen years ago.

MSC
Roslyn, New York
November 29, 2019
א׳ דר״ח כסלו תש״פ הוא יום השנה הארבעים לפטירת אמי מורתי ע״ה וז״ל

Chapter One

The First Gate

Knowing God

For more than a millennium, it has become traditional for Jewish authors to describe the quest for spiritual fulfillment as a pilgrim's journey leading those who undertake it through a series of gates set into the concentric walls that surround a great—and otherwise totally inaccessible—palace. But although the image thus conjured up is obviously meant metaphorically to describe an individual's spiritual growth, the slow passage through the gates is almost always described nonetheless as a real journey characterized, like all real journeys, by chartable trajectory and attainable destination . . . and almost never as an abstruse exercise in poetic thinking divorced from the physical reality of the world. This being the case, the traveler is generally depicted as an actual wayfarer who reasonably hopes to arrive, at least eventually, at an actual place.

Over the centuries, authors who chose to frame their descriptions of the redemptive journey as this kind of passage through a series of concentric walls have vied with each other to identify, and even to name, the specific gates in those walls through which pilgrims must pass on their journey to God. Some of their efforts have withstood the test of time and their works—the great classics of Jewish spiritual literature—are read and studied, at least in some circles, even today. Others have failed to retain their popularity and are read, to the extent they are read at all, by students of spiritual literature rather than by people intent on learning from them how they might personally embark on such a journey. Possessed of the conviction that every generation should feel challenged to identify its own set of gates, and perhaps even that every individual ought do so, I have written this book to propose to would-be travelers a set of ten gates through which to consider passing on the way to attaining the great goal of all human spiritual endeavor: the quest for redemption in God characterized by uncompromised, unyielding allegiance to the absolute integrity of the moral intellect.

There is no great need to quibble over the precise order in which these gates are presented or even over the specific names I have assigned to each. Nor, although these gates are the ones I have personally attempted to traverse on my own spiritual journey, do readers need to assume that my path must necessarily also be theirs. Indeed, the details presented in this book are rooted in my own journey solely because all honest theology is necessarily some version of its author's spiritual autobiography.

And so we begin with the first gate of all, the gate of knowing God. Like all of the gates, this one is fashioned, not of bricks or stones, but of puzzles and paradoxes that reason dictates ought to be unresolvable. But the very fact that paradoxes that cannot be resolved can be embraced nevertheless is a truth no less relevant here than it is in the sphere of romantic love . . . as is the fact also that the pilgrim willing to devote sufficient energy to knowing the unknowable can, in the end, at least come to know something. In turn, that *something* can stand in for whatever hides behind the shield of unresolvable paradox and un-unravelable riddle and become—in its own inexplicable yet highly utilitarian way—a useful paving stone on the pilgrim's path toward a personal Jerusalem.

Scripture stresses over and over that God may not be known. That much seems simple to accept . . . and yet the same Bible that harps endlessly on the fact that the ineffable nature of God can never be seized by mortals also commands the faithful to love God with all their hearts, with all their souls, and with all their might. That too sounds reasonable, except for the crucial flaw that the same human beings commanded to love God are generally *also* incapable of conceiving of what it would (or even could) mean to give themselves totally and absolutely to lovers they have not personally encountered in the context of their day-to-day lives and whom they therefore do not actually know at all.

And so we come to the great paradox that looms large at the very outset of the pilgrim's journey: that the heart that yearns for God must come to transcend its own nature in a way that ought logically—and wholly reasonably—to be impossible, and totally so. Yet, as noted, paradox that cannot be resolved can nonetheless be embraced . . . and the first step would-be pilgrims must take toward God must, therefore, involve their willingness to embrace the possible/impossible notion of knowing the unknowable God without hiding behind a shield of pious slogans and glib platitudes. The wall, almost by definition, cannot be scaled. But, of course, a wall with a gate set in it does not *need* to be scaled at all.

THE FIRST STEP IS THE HARDEST

The first step on the journey—the hardest and most distressing, but also the most liberating and inspiring step a human being can take toward spiritual fulfillment, toward redemption—is to accept, and to accept wholeheartedly and without any inner reservation whatsoever, that every single word ever written—or spoken aloud or even conceived of in thought—that every single *idea* any human being has ever formulated about God or about any aspect of God's existence is, by definition, a *midrash*—a kind of commentary—on divine reality as it exists unencumbered by the strictures of language, image, and symbol . . . and that there are no exceptions to this principle of any sort whatsoever nor is it conceivable that there ever could be any. Accepting this idea—and internalizing its various implications and ramifications—will be disorienting and upsetting for most who hold religion in esteem. Nonetheless, any who reject this idea and insist that they actually *can* seize the nature of God merely by insisting repeatedly and forcefully that they somehow possess the ability intellectually and spiritually to transcend the metaphoric and symbolic language of Scripture and to fathom the unfathomable reality behind even the least obscure God talk—such people cannot be said to know God, or even really to know *of* God, in any but the least meaningful way possible. Nor can it be supposed that the prayers of such people—addressed as they inevitably must be to a concept of God that is little more than a figment of their imaginations—can bear interpretation other than as poetic expressions of their own personal needs and private desires. This, in a nutshell, is the whole Torah and the rest, mere *midrash*. But the study of *midrash* can be productive in its own right, and also very gratifying and satisfying.

UNKNOWN AND UNKNOWABLE

This really isn't a journey for the timid. For most people, in fact, it will be disorienting and upsetting even to imagine what it would be like to approach God in an atmosphere of absolute honesty and total candor, let alone actually to do so. What *is* easy, on the other hand, is to be crippled by the absurdity inherent in the notion of entering into any kind of relationship at all, let alone one characterized by caring and love, with a God who cannot logically be known in the way people generally know each other and of each other. In a sense, this is the bedrock issue with which every individual possessed of real spiritual aspirations has to grapple and eventually come to terms. Yet in this, like in so many things, the bottom line is that reality trumps paradox . . . and the fact that there are individuals who do manage to transcend the limits of their own human intellects precisely by acknowledging those limits and then by refusing to lie about them is far more significant than might seem at first.

Because there is something of the way human lovers learn how to love by loving in the way the aspiring faithful are called upon to learn to believe by believing, Scripture uses the language of love to describe the kind of relationship that may exist between a human being and the unknowable God . . . and also subtly to suggest that the effort to know God, just like the effort to love another person, will always be derailed by egotism and unearned self-pride.

For Jews, the paving stones that lie along the path to God will always be the commandments of the Torah. But here too, it is key to remember that the Lover is not so much unknown as unknowable . . . and that the quest for love will therefore always be carried out within the realm of myth and metaphor. Because the effort to love God is so often described in language that derives from the framework of mutual desire and acquiescence that characterizes the intimacy of earthly lovers, for example, those who embrace the commandments of the Torah as their path to God often speak as though their actions were able to satisfy some one or another of God's needs or desires. This is not at all unreasonable, but it is also true that love between the would-be person of faith and God cannot flourish any more successfully in an atmosphere of unacknowledged metaphor than ever could the love of human lovers. Therefore, any who perform the commandments—including even the simplest and least arduous among them—out of the conviction that God "wants" them to do this or that thing end up disabling their ability to move forward on the path toward redemption *in* God because they have attributed desire and want—and hence imperfection—*to* God.

The basic principle always to bear in mind is that the attribution of desire to God is at best a metaphor meant to suggest the possibility of love. To insist on the literal truth of those scriptural passages that speak about God wanting this or that thing, therefore, is to miss the point almost entirely and this, I suspect, is the true meaning of the words slightly pathetically spoken by King Ahab to the prophet Micaiah, "How many times must I adjure you to speak to me only truth in the name of God?" (1 Kings 22:16 and 2 Chronicles 18:15). Like the search for love, the spiritual quest cannot be carried out successfully, even some of the time, in the context of willful self-delusion.

RENOUNCING CHUTZPAH

In earliest times, the ancestors of the Jewish people took to using the name "God" to refer to the moral core of absolute existence that rests beneath, beyond, and behind the perceptible universe. Through the medium of its daughter religions, Islam and Christianity, this linguistic usage spread throughout the Western world, but, for all it has become widespread, it still cannot be deemed to state an absolute truth. Indeed, any effort to delimit the power and majesty of the divine by encasing it within either words or mental images must be adjudicated flawed, thus at least in some sense false, and this is what the prophet meant when he asked, simply and rhetorically: "To whom would you compare God?" (Isaiah 40:18). To whom indeed!

It follows, therefore, that any in this world who unambiguously characterize this or that mode of behavior as being or not being in accordance with God's will are behaving at least slightly fraudulently . . . and this is true no matter how much simpler such people's lives would be if otherwise were to be the case. The bottom line is this: although no human being may know God plainly, only those courageous enough to admit as much in their hearts can claim to be counted among those who even know *of* God. Giving forth with self-serving certainty about things regarding which certainty of any sort is impossible is unjustifiable chutzpah. On the other hand, accepting the limits of human perception is the first step any of us can take toward salvation in God. Indeed, accepting this principle is probably the most difficult of first steps any can take on the journey to Jerusalem . . . and lying about it, the most seductive of self-serving falsehoods.

DECENCY AND DEPRAVITY

And there's another paradox to consider as well, one that lives at the heart of the matter: knowing *of* God is only knowing God when it is not confused, consciously or unintentionally, with *actually* knowing God. It is natural enough, after all, that anyone who observes the goings-on in our violent, unjust world for long enough will eventually yearn to believe that there is some invisible, yet wholly real, force that governs the world and its people and its things . . . and that this yearned-for force, however it is named or described, has the potential to grant order and meaning to the lives people live. Then, learning (as the would-be faithful eventually do) that this force of order and governance rooted in ethical morality is described in the Bible as God, it is all too natural to take that hopeful identification as a simple fact rather than as an expression of the same yearning for God on the part of the ancients that even today stimulates spiritual endeavor on the part of moderns.

Yet, for all that the longing for God may surely be real in the hearts of the faithful, it is *still* the case that religion can never thrive in an atmosphere of pious self-delusion. Therefore, in the absolute absence of unambiguous evidence, any who insist on identifying God with this mysterious, evasive force they can neither locate nor describe (and the existence of which they cannot verify even *un*convincingly) are guilty—to say the very least—of lying about God.

To hope, to yearn, to theorize, to dream . . . these are all the tools of people who wish for goodness in the world and none of them needs to be justified at all. To allow yourself, on the other hand, to give voice to those dreams and hopes for justice in the world by asserting things about God that, in the absence of convincing evidence, could just as easily be false as true is to flee, like Jonah in his day, from the very God you claim so ardently to be seeking. Saying you know God without *actually* knowing God is to behave like children who brag to their classmates that they know a movie star or a sports hero they've never actually met because it is impossible for them to imagine that individual *not* being as imagined by such loyal and devoted fans as themselves. Making similar claims about God is no less a lie for being easily understandable and also no less congruent with the path of spiritual integrity than any would-be lover's lie, no matter how flattering, would be with anyone's effort to establish a true and permanent bond of love with another.

MAKING YOUR OWN BRICKS

While we're on the subject of lies, the biggest, fattest one they told you as a child was how much fun the practice of religion was going to be. Your teachers surely meant well, but the truth is that religion is frustrating, maddening, and exasperating. Spiritual progress is measurable—to the extent it can be measured at all—in millimeters, not miles. The possibility of swerving off into craziness is not only real, but *so* real as to be a genuine risk for most of the people most of the time. Of the ten thousand worst crimes committed by human beings, I shudder to think how many have been motivated by religion and justified with reference to faith in God.

A good jumping-off point, then, is to accept from the onset that the possibility of failure *always* exists. To make matters worse, the reasons people fail in the pursuit of their own spiritual goals are almost invariably by-products of their own inability to harness their native intelligence in the pursuit of the faith they claim so ardently to be seeking. And, indeed, although there are stumbling blocks on the spiritual path so numerous that nobody moves forward without tripping over at least some of them, the single biggest stumbling block of all is the kind of pernicious arrogance that leads people to insist that there is certainty where only uncertainty actually exists, or that there exists unassailable truth where it is inconceivable that any absolute truth even *could* ever exist, let alone that it actually does.

There are no such things as pious, therefore justifiable, lies about God. And, as a result, there is no wall higher than the wall people build between themselves and God with bricks fashioned of arrogance and eagerly embraced fantasy.

When the Bible says that "the yearning of the pious is a delight" (Proverbs 10:28), it is referring to the kind of yearning on the part of a human being rooted in an unwavering commitment to honesty and absolute intellectual integrity. Indeed, it is a cardinal principle of principled faith that any (and every) effort to know God through the medium of unproven theories embraced as self-evident facts is doomed to failure, and this surely is what the psalmist meant by writing in God's name that "the fraudulent shall not sit in the midst of My house / nor shall liars be established before Me" (Psalm 101:7).

THE LANGUAGE OF GOD

There are some relatively unpalatable facts we all must embrace if we truly wish to approach, let alone successfully to pass through, the gate of the knowledge of God. I've already mentioned several of them, but the toughest of them all to digest is the simple fact that people *invariably* conceive of God according to the givens of the world in which they live and that, as a result, there can be no absolute truth in anything spoken, or even thought, about God in any human language that is a byproduct of the cultural milieu in which it developed. (Regretfully, this includes all human languages.) Therefore, any who blithely convey the "word of God" in any language at all must be considered, at best, as presenting a report on their personal experience of the communicative presence of the divine. No less than that, assuming the integrity of the speaker . . . but also no more. The implications of this thought alone for someone attempting to seek God along the path of ritual and rite should be staggering. Are you *not* staggered? Perhaps you should read this paragraph again a bit more slowly!

To the extent that it is reasonable to interpret the experience of God's communicative presence by describing it in words, it is legitimate to speak of God as speaking in a specific language . . . but logic dictates that God must *always* be presumed to have spoken to the individual in question in a private, totally idiosyncratic language that pertains to that specific person, not to that person's nation or ethnic group . . . and which only that person, therefore, is capable of interpreting even cursorily.

This phenomenon—the use of the words of a known language to speak in a private, idiosyncratic code to another—will be familiar to most from the realm of romantic love. And the notion that the use of words to create a path toward spiritual communion is like the use of language between human lovers will likely be resonant for another reason as well: because the intimacy of lovers is specifically *not* expressed by the invention of a new language *per se*, but by the use of language to create a private lovers' universe of intimate discourse, a world in which language becomes a private code invested with deep, personal meaning only the two who reside there share or may share. In that sense, it may be considered reasonable for the individual possessed of spiritual integrity to speak of God speaking . . . but the word of God is neither speech nor language and has therefore neither grammar nor syntax. It cannot be analyzed or searched for secret codes or ciphers. To the extent it exists at all, it is a kiss, not a word; melody, not lyric; substance, not form.

Every effort to find traces of God's existence in this world through the use of language must therefore be considered a kind of noble experiment that can only succeed when it is accepted—and accepted absolutely—that it cannot possibly succeed. Perhaps the closest humans can come to seizing the concept is through the contemplation of instrumental music, a *kind* of language capable of inducing intense emotion and of eliciting profound response without the use of words at all. Yet, for all its profundity, music is basically content-neutral and even Beethoven himself could not have used a newly composed melody to send detailed information to a plumber, say, about the need for specific repairs to the pipes beneath the Schwarzspanierhaus. In the end, it is probably a better idea for the faithful simply to accept that the language of God, like the discourse of lovers, is no language and all languages, speech outside of talking, words outside of sound. The word of God can indeed be expressed in the languages of the world, but the relationship between the word of God and the words of God found in the Bible is the same as the relationship between an apple and a photograph of an apple . . . or perhaps between that apple and the most exquisite painting of an apple imaginable, one that, despite the degree to which the intelligence, passion, skill, and deep emotion of the artist are totally invested in its brush strokes, would still not be an actual apple even if it were somehow ingested by some daring soul hoping to come to know what apples are through the experience.

LYING ABOUT GOD

Lying is inimical to the search for the knowledge of God even when the lies take the form of pious platitudes or soothing slogans. People, therefore, who begin sentences with the words "I believe" and then finish those sentences with ideas that can neither be proven with certainty nor even demonstrated to be true beyond reasonable doubt cannot be supposed to be speaking wholly honestly. (What such people mean to say, or ought to mean to say, is that they wish to believe—or wish they could believe—in the truth of whatever it is they are saying.) If such speakers are giving forth on the nature of God, however, then they are guilty of ignoring the ancient lesson of Rabbi Ḥanina to the effect that the signet seal of the blessed Holy One is Truth itself . . . and that is not at all a good plan for people seeking meaningful spiritual growth. (Rabbi Ḥanina's comment is preserved in the Talmud at B. Shabbat 55a, Yoma 69b, and Sanhedrin 64a.)

There are those who speak falsely about God out of frustration and naiveté . . . but there are also those who do so by building elaborate spiritual lives on foundations fashioned of impossible beliefs and unlikely, unprovable theories. Of these, two of the most widespread are the notion that the details of divine existence change and develop from generation to generation in accordance with the will of specific individuals that God be this or that thing or behave in this or that way, and the theory that worshipers through their efforts somehow acquire the right to insist that God behave in some specific manner that corresponds to their personal needs or wants. The Bible qualifies people who embrace either of these beliefs as "the stubborn of heart" because they simply cannot abide the fact that they cannot will God to react or respond to them or their activities—and also because, when frustrated by their inability to make reality conform to their own wishes, such people conduct themselves as though such were the case anyway. In our society, we tend to indulge spoiled children, but the Bible teaches that "the stubborn of heart are an abomination before God" (Proverbs 11:20) and that, surely, is as self-evident as it is succinctly put. The good news is that it is entirely possible to seek out God without becoming stubborn of heart, directionless, beliefless, faithless, or devoid of spiritual bearing. The bad news is that it is also *entirely* possible to be all of the above . . . and still widely to be considered a walking paradigm of piety.

FAITH

As noted above, faith is the great suit of armor beloved by those who conduct their religious lives without acknowledging even the possibility of pursuing spiritual growth in an atmosphere of intellectual and emotional integrity. Nonetheless, there really *is* no such thing as making something so by insisting that you believe in it and, in the end, everybody really does know that. As a result, any who claim that they believe with all their soul and with all their heart and with all their might in notions and ideas about God that cannot possible be verified—and which, therefore, as far as they know, could also be totally false—are using the concept of faith to distance themselves from God and, especially, from the love of God.

It is surely the case that there are many who admire people who speak openly and enthusiastically about faith, but the Bible itself is less indulgent of wishful thinking translated into the language of religion. When, for example, the Book of Proverbs warns sternly against "selling the truth," it means to warn against what we would call selling *out* the truth by insisting that a distinction between scientific and spiritual truth exists in a real enough way to make reasonable the claim that a thinking person *can* actually know things about God that that same individual has neither experienced personally nor tested scientifically. And it also means that it is never even slightly reasonable to embrace spiritual truths wholeheartedly without knowing if they correspond to actual reality. That no sane person would take this approach with respect to the physical universe only makes the Bible's admonition more pathetic, however, not any less sharp.

As a kind of spiritual exercise, I suggest this: for once, allow yourself to say bluntly how things are. You don't have to say it aloud—speaking these truths in the privacy of your own heart is certainly good enough—but taking this challenge to heart means accepting that honest worship cannot take place in the absence of an unfettered intellect and a spirit permitted to flourish in an atmosphere of total intellectual candor, and this point the prophet made almost three millennia ago by speaking in God's name and declaring that "My people is being destroyed through a lack of intellect, for you have been revolted by intellectuality. Therefore shall I too be revolted—too revolted to let you to serve Me" (Hosea 4:6). Those are, or should be, chilling words. But, upsetting though they may be, the prophet's words can nonetheless serve as an excellent mantra for people taking their first steps toward God. My counsel would be to memorize those words and let them guide you forward toward accepting as fully logical the supposition that God, who is the Truth of the world, will almost surely disdain the efforts of worshipers undertaken other than in the context of total honesty. For people trained from childhood to expect God to respond to even the most pathetic attempts at worship with unrestrained divine delight, this should be—to say the very least—a sobering thought.

All the above notwithstanding, faith itself is not the enemy of all religion—only the self-righteous variety. And, indeed, there is also another kind of faith in the world, the kind that grants life to people who possess it and makes alive those who embrace it without causing them any harm at all. It is the kind of faith by which the righteous live—as Scripture says, "the righteous individual lives by his faith" (Habakkuk 2:4)—and the embrace of which constitutes the first step toward the knowledge of God that anyone can take. This is the kind of faith people maintain in things that they know to be true and which they can verify *as* true when the processes of sensory perception and intellectual deduction join together to form a kind of bridge between the inner soul of an individual and the outer world in which that individual lives and functions. In a world that has elevated self-delusion to an art form, this kind of faith is nonetheless totally devoid of fraud and fantasy, and it is wholly and utterly honest. In ancient times, this was the faith of Abraham, whom Scripture (at Genesis 15:6) says was considered fully righteous precisely because his faith was not built on a foundation of pious lies or self-serving fantasies, but on the patriarch's empirically verifiable experience of the reality of the living God. In the end, all perception is *midrash* . . . but the faith of Abraham remains, generation after generation, not so much as a prize to be claimed, but a challenge to be embraced by those possessed of sufficient courage actually to run the race—as opposed to sitting comfortably in the bleachers and proudly declaring the race won.

EMBRACING UNANSWERABILITY

Another stumbling block on the path to the knowledge of God is the pedant's need to intellectualize regarding things that can only be understood experientially. Yet the same world that would *never* grant much credence to a scientist who never enters a laboratory but instead chooses merely to sit in a room somewhere and think about the natural world grants nothing *but* credence to people in the religious world who do just that with respect to the knowledge of God. This is merely another way that society, for all it pays lip service to the worth of religion, actually marginalizes it by looking away when people who trumpet unverifiable, hence unverified, notions as though they were self-evident axioms parade around as paradigms of religiosity without anyone daring to ask how they know the "truths" they declaim actually to be true.

An infant suckles at its mother's breast and enjoys the succor, warmth, and nourishment that inheres in the experience without pausing to wonder where the breast came from or to worry if it might someday vanish. As far as we can manage it, we should scruple to relate to God in more or less the same way such babies relates to their mothers: as the source of our spiritual and physical nourishment and succor in the world—and as our sole, permanent, unshakable source of ultimate support in a world of danger and uncertainty—without ruining the experience by drenching it in worries about where, precisely, our faith comes from and what will happen someday if it somehow vanishes. This is not the negation of what I've written above about spiritual integrity, only its slightly upsetting corollary: the *honest* experience of emotion is not by its nature *dishonest*. (How could it be?) What *is* dishonest, however, is insisting that an emotion honestly experienced is something *other* than all it ever can be: the perception of feeling within the human heart.

We human beings should never weaken our ability to experience the love of God by asking a never-ending series of questions that have no answers and will never have any. Embracing the unanswerability of specific questions does not constitute an abandonment of spiritual integrity, however, and merely signals a willingness on the part of an individual to accept that the human intellect has limits . . . and that it is inevitable that even the most ardently religious individual is going to come up short in terms of at least *some* answers to at least *some* questions when attempting to contemplate the reality of a God whom logic dictates must exist beyond the limits of human perception. Spiritual integrity is honesty, not arrogance.

There is a huge and awesome difference between people who make up answers to difficult or upsetting questions by claiming to possess secret knowledge that no one else knows or can access . . . and people who consciously decide to bask in the glow of God's earthly presence without becoming completely and ruinously enmeshed in questions that, because they have no answers, can only overwhelm the experience of seeing the light of God's face shining forth into the world. Admitting that such an experience by its very nature lies outside the boundaries of language and beyond the limits of comprehension, however, is not lying about God.

WHATEVER LEADS TO FAITH IS A BLESSING

People who seek to know God through the medium of worship and obedience to the laws of Scripture certainly do not hope for God to respond to their efforts by sending them illness or weakness of body, spirit, or soul. Nonetheless, there are people in the world who first become aware of God's presence in their lives and in the world precisely when they feel ill or weak . . . and for such people infirmity can serve as a personal path forward toward spiritual awareness, toward faith, toward Jerusalem. Indeed, one of the foundational ideas upon which religion pursued with spiritual integrity rests is that anything at all that brings people to know God, or even to know *of* God, is at least a kind of a blessing.

Therefore, there is no logic at all to the loathing and fear of sickness which, when they do experience it, so many use as some sort of proof positive that God clearly must have no interest whatsoever in their welfare. Logic suggests that God uses all the things people fear the most in the world in precisely the same way chefs use wooden mallets to soften up beef before grilling it . . . and also to challenge people to find the inner spiritual strength *not* to hold anything in disdain that has the ability to lead them to God. In the end, no sane person wishes for illness . . . but how can anything that inspires reliance on God be a sign, let alone proof, of divine apathy? When the author of the Book of Judges depicts Samson as noting that sweetness can come forth from the roughest and least likely point of origin (Judges 14:14), what he means to say that the seeds of faith can be sown in even the least overtly fertile soil. In the vegetable market, of course, shoppers judge the carrots on their own merits without caring at all about—or bothering even to inquire about—the soil in which they originally grew.

THE PRISM OF BEHOLDENNESS

There are those who come to know God through the medium, not so much of worship or obedience, but of gratitude. Indeed, there are those who bless God for all the good things in their lives in accordance with the psalmist's injunction to "give thanks to God for divine mercy and for the wondrous way God acts in people's lives" (Psalm 107:8–9) and there is certainly nothing at all wrong with coming to God through the medium of the gratitude you may well feel for all the good things and blessings in your life. Nor is there any lack of spiritual integrity in the cultivation of the kind of deep, abiding gratitude that leads to a productive sense of God's reality as focused through the prism of beholdenness.

There *is* an issue of integrity here, however, and it has to do with the unsettling set of corollaries such honest emotions bring along—or *should* bring along—in their logical wake. Those, for example, who say that they consider themselves blessed by God when they experience success or great joy can only *really* come to know God through those sentiments of gratitude if they are also ready to say with complete sincerity that all the suffering that comes into their lives—and all the instances of failure and unwarranted *un*-happiness they encounter—that all of those experiences are *also* rooted in God's governance of the world.

The message is a bit dour, but the logic is impeccable: those who believe in God as the Author only of those bits of history they find appealing cannot be said to believe in any meaningful way in the God depicted in the pages of Scripture as the source of ongoing moral governance in the physical world. This is such an unpalatable truth that the ancient liturgist who created the first blessing recited as part of the Evening Service took the verse from Isaiah with which he wished to work (Isaiah 45:7, "[I am the] Fashioner of light and the Creator of darkness, the Maker of peace and the Creator of evil—I, God, am the Doer of all these things") and edited it to acknowledge God rather blandly instead as the Maker of Peace and the Creator of all things. Why someone creating a liturgical benediction would do such a thing is easy to explain and even easier to rationalize. But the liturgist's theological timidity didn't and doesn't make Isaiah's oracle any less true.

THE OUTER EDGE OF GOD

Logic is the bedrock on which the knowledge of God must rest . . . and this is so in every context and at all times. Logic, for example, requires that we imagine God as existing beyond the boundaries of time and space . . . and this is the meaning of the famous question Zophar the Naamathite puts to Job, "Can you find the boundary of God? Can you locate the outermost edge of the Almighty?" (Job 11:7). But for all the Naamathite's questions were rhetorical and their answers obvious, his point was and is still disorienting: if God exists without reference to the spatial or temporal physics of the created universe, then God cannot be said to exist in terms of width or height or length—or time—at all, let alone be measurable by humans incapable even of *conceiving* of non-spatial space that somehow also exists outside the framework of inexorably ongoing time.

However, it must also be acknowledged that the very same human logic that *requires* us to think of God as existing outside of time and space also *prevents* us—or at least those of us untrained in quantum physicists—from attributing any real meaning to the notion of existence outside of time and space. Nonetheless, for all it may well be impossible to seize the concept, to insist that God exists within the boundaries of spatial, time-bound reality is to lie about God and this was possibly the real point of Zophar's rhetorical questions: to stress that the puniness of the human intellect cannot be used to justify lying about God no matter *how* disorienting—or upsetting—the resultant truth, or lack of truth, may be.

Spiritual integrity is truth, not arrogance. On the one hand, to assert the notion of divine existence outside of time and space as though it were a concept plainly put, thus easily seized, is to imprison the reality of God's presence on earth in a steel mesh of slogans and empty platitudes. But this is also true: to seek God in the context of total spiritual integrity means to search for traces of the divine in the innermost chambers of a human heart that trembles *precisely* with the creative tension that results from any effort to contemplate the exquisite riddle of divine existence in the non-divine world. And, just as in the realm of romantic love, impossibility yields its own possibilities. Indeed, when Scripture reports that God said to Moses, "I am what I am" (Exodus 3:14), the point can only be for readers to imagine God revealing a truth no less simple than inscrutable: "The nature of My being is peculiar to Me alone," the greatest of all prophets understood God to be saying, "for I exist in a way totally different from the way you do. Yet, somehow the very fact that the same thing can be said of Me and you—that we both exist—creates at least the possibility of interaction, even if it is impossible that the word 'exist' itself could possible mean the same thing when applied to us both."

NOT LIGHT

Spiritual integrity cannot exist in the context of unacknowledged metaphor, but speaking about God in an "as-if" way can still be useful . . . when it is openly acknowledged that such is the case *and* that the speaker has chosen to step into the realm of literary symbolism precisely to make a point that would otherwise remain inexpressible. For example, it might be useful for some to think of God as a great surge of light or as a kind of physically nonexistent reality made totally of light, and this is reflected in many verses of Scripture as, for example, "God is my light" (Psalm 27:1) or "God shall be a light to me" (Micah 7:8) or "and to you shall God be an everlasting light" (Isaiah 60:19).

The notion of God self-manifesting in the world as a being made wholly of light, however, will only be useful to those who remember to remember that it is utterly untrue, that God is neither light nor made of light, that light itself is a created thing, as is unambiguously taught in the Torah: "And God said, 'Let there be light' and there was light" (Genesis 1:3). Moreover, light is an existent thing—and existence is a word we can use to describe God in the world only if we are prepared to deprive the word of any meaning at all . . . or rather of any meaning that human beings can fathom, which more or less comes to the same thing.

Likening the notion of needing faith in God adequately to interpret and decipher the world to the simple idea of needing light to see makes perfect sense. Declaring that the reality of God is no more affected by atheists' lack of faith than is the reality of light by the existence of blind people also makes good sense. Real yet without physicality, existent yet unfettered by the natural laws that govern most other existent things, perceptible yet not fully visible absent the presence of the lighted thing—light exists in the world in a way that suggests how God exists in the world and rooting faith in that set of helpful images and ideas is perfectly legitimate and reasonable. Nor is speaking about God with reference to the things of the world inherently blasphemous or pointless. Just to the contrary, lyrical speech about God can be useful and helpful in assisting human beings to say anything at all about a God who exists outside the rubrics of fathomable reality. Through the contemplation of the world, human beings can indeed come to God—this is the simple meaning of the psalmist's famous words, "In Your light, we see light" (Psalm 36:10)—but the ability to step closer to faith by likening God to this or that thing is only meaningful when the individual involved openly acknowledges the nature of the process . . . and is disabled totally when that individual begins arrogantly to insist that he or she knows something of God plainly, that God *is* this or that thing.

TOWARD THE PRIVATE JERUSALEM

Part of the secret of living a life of spiritual integrity involves losing the natural fear of unresolved—and unresolvable—paradox most people bring to their quests for God. Indeed, when properly and openly acknowledged, the tension that inheres in even the most maddening paradox can propel the pilgrim forward along the path toward knowing God along the finite-infinite landscape of human perceptive consciousness, a process that can lead such a person successfully to grapple with concepts that cannot be reconciled with each other yet both of which must necessarily be absolutely true.

To step into this almost impenetrable thicket of worrisome paradox without becoming overwhelmed and disoriented, we would all do well to resolve to precede every act of worship—every commandment fulfilled, every prayer spoken or whispered, every ritual performed, even every act of kindness undertaken as an expression of personal piety—with a few words from the Psalms: *elohim lanu maḥaseh va·oz / ezrah b'tzarot nimtza me·od* (Psalm 46:2). The words mean this: "God is our haven and our strength / a source of help, fully present in times of trouble." The key words are *nimtza me·od*, the Hebrew for "fully present." Not "vaguely existent." Not "theoretically real." Not "more or less there" (and, it seems, always more less than more.) But "fully present"—just as you yourself must be when you lift up your heart in prayer and address God either in word or deed. Fully present means just what it sounds like it must mean—that the whole point of calling out to God in times of trouble, of laboring to come to think of God as a source of strength and as a haven—the whole point of all that effort is to accept God as fully present in your life. Forget that and you become the spiritual equivalent of individuals who attempt to find true love in their lives by reading romance novels.

Consider, for example, that it is both totally reasonable *and* totally impossible to assert that existence and nonexistence meet and become identical in the same God whose existence in the world can only be asserted by denying the term any meaning at all and which can be only described—and then only within the realm of poetry and metaphor—as an endlessly swirling vortex of illusion and reality mixed together in an electrified whirlwind of absolute being and unqualified nothingness. From accepting the impossibility of resolving the riddle of divine existence, however, can come a conclusion that is *fully* possible to accept: that, in the end, God can neither be known nor comprehended, only sensed—occasionally—for the length of the briefest of moments by solitary travelers making their slow, painful progress forward on secret roads that lead through the inmost chambers of those individuals' hearts to their private Jerusalems, to the World beyond the world, to the Life beyond life, to God.

THE CORE OF EVERY COMMANDMENT

The notion that the path toward personal redemption begins with the willingness of an individual to submit to the rule of God is the Bible's single most foundational idea. This does not mean, however, that God becomes accessible in some magical way to people who do this or that thing at some pre-appointed time or who say some specific prayer in some pre-ordained way. That much may seem obvious, but trying actually to define the exact way God becomes even conditionally knowable through the medium of submission to divine law is dramatically less simple a task that those used to knuckling under to its exigencies generally permit themselves to think.

To say the same thing in specifically Jewish terms, the commandments of the Torah are the rituals that define the spiritual quest. They are the building blocks, the steppingstones, the specific *things* people do to progress along their private spiritual paths to faith in God. But harping endlessly on the duty of the individual to obey the laws of Scripture and explaining how, precisely, obedience to those laws will bring that person closer to God are two entirely different things. Indeed, no one who would know God, or even *of* God, through the medium of obedience to the laws of Scripture can step away from the responsibility of explaining, to themselves if to no one else, how precisely obedience to the laws of the Bible leads to spiritual progress.

I don't really understand how my computer works, but I know that it's in working order because, at least mostly, it does what I wish it to do when I follow certain specific procedures and press the keys in certain, learned ways. I could say the same about my cell phone—that I can say with certainty that it works even without understanding exactly how I can talk into a little piece of molded plastic and be heard by someone driving along on the road between Jerusalem and Tel Aviv. Those are assertions I can make and mean because I don't feel the need to understand precisely how a machine works to feel able to say that it is in working order. But can I say the same about religion?

When divested of the magic qualities people seem almost invariably predisposed to attribute to them, the commandments of the Torah may best be visualized as elaborate planets of ritual rotating endlessly around the central ideas that roil and churn deep inside their ideational cores. But, for all it is the rituals themselves that are evocative and intriguing, it is specifically and only the ideas that generate them which grant meaning to their performance and which, therefore, transform them all from gratuitous efforts magically to subdue the world—and to pressure God into responding generously to specific needs and wants—into sacred acts of divine worship. Moreover, it is specifically in this way that the commandments of Scripture function effectively in the spiritual lives of the faithful: even though it is impossible to imagine even the most scrupulously observant human being coming to know God through the normal processes of sensory perception people use to perceive, decode, and decipher the world, the Torah nevertheless returns over and over to the idea that an individual may learn to know God—or at least to know *of* God—by internalizing the ideas that rest at the core of each commandment. And it is through the performance of these commandments according to all the detailed minutiae of the system of law Jews call *halakhah* that those ideas may be accessed the most profoundly, thus granting them the deepest meaning possible in the real-time lives of actual people.

Although it is ultimately true that there are as many of these ideas as there are commandments, it is also the case that many of these commandments are interrelated precisely by having interrelated ideas at their respective cores. There are not, therefore, an unlimited number of ideas that Scripture wishes to propose to the faithful as notions about God capable of serving as the framework for a life-long quest to perceive God within the textured folds of human life. Indeed, some of these ideas come so regularly to the fore as to suggest themselves as the principal principles of faith. In turn, these specific ideas are able to transcend their original scriptural role as the ideational cores of specific commandments and become the principles of faith the pious will seek to embrace more generally through meditative contemplation and through study. Of course, different readers will number different ideas among these central pillars of faith, but it seems to me that there are basically seven principles that serve as the foundation stones upon which stands the elaborate ideational edifice in which the Bible invites the faithful to seek lives in God, just as Scripture says of Wisdom at Proverbs 9:1 that she builds her palace upon seven pillars. (Does she always? Even asking the question is to miss the point.)

Yet, for all their depth and complexity, these seven pillars of faith can be stated plainly and directly. God is the creator of the world and of all humanity. God is the cosmic, all-powerful source of freedom and liberation in the world. God is the Holy One of Israel and the source of holiness in the world. God is the owner of the cosmic house that is the universe and thus the divine host of all who live in the world as guests sheltering for a long night under somebody else's roof. God is a just judge who judges the world with scrupulous fairness and honesty. God is the heart of the world and the source of love in it. God is the source of morality and goodness, the ground of being as viewed through the prism of uncompromising ethical rectitude. There are others, of course . . . but these are the central tenets of faith that I discern behind the ritual life recommended by Scripture as the framework for a life lived purposefully and well, the seven pillars upon which wisdom rests, the seven ideas that the commandments of Scripture taken as a whole exist to inculcate into the consciousnesses of the would-be faithful.

THE QUEST FOR DIVINE COMFORT

It all comes down to candor and humility. The cornerstone of every honest attempt to live a life in and of God must, almost by definition, be the profound conviction that it is beyond the ability of human beings to understand the concept of divinity fully or to seize precisely how God functions effectively in a world that cannot possibly contain even some infinitesimal fraction of divine reality. There is, therefore, something both irrational and misguided about people who complain petulantly that the performance of some specific commandment failed to provide them with the superhuman ability to know God through its agency and that it may therefore be dispensed with by the rationally pious despite its scriptural pedigree.

The commandments are not magic keys to the knowledge of God, but rather opportunities for human beings to identify some specific avenue to faith they might otherwise have left unnoticed, hence untraveled, and then, through the observance of that particular commandment, to travel it. The commandments cannot change the nature of the universe. They cannot make the elusive God of Israel pop up into the lives of people the way switching on a television set brings newscasters and talk show hosts into the living rooms of the people in whose homes those television sets are located. In the end, the commandments cannot *do* anything at all, *except*—and this is a huge "except"—*except* make slightly wider and deeper the human hearts of those who embrace them in the hope of finding God through the medium of worship. Nothing more. But also nothing less.

The commandments do not magically usher people into the presence of God, but they do possess the uncanny ability to assist the people who embrace them in finding traces of God's reality in the details of their everyday lives. And this too is key: through obedience to the commandments, it becomes reasonable to imagine that we just might, at least eventually, succeed at opening our eyes at precisely the right moment to gaze for the briefest of seconds at the splendor of the divine that hides behind and beyond the landscape of the world. Indeed, it is precisely this experience of being fully present and totally aware when the portals of heaven fleetingly open and the potential to know God presents itself for a passing second or two that the ancients called the redemption of the individual. But the fact that the race is run in a matter of seconds doesn't make it less necessary for those who would win it to train for years in advance.

It is also possible not to win at all, even after long years of training, because any race that may be won may also be lost. Every athlete knows this dour truth perfectly well, but the lesson seems dramatically harder to accept in the religious context. More's the pity, actually, because coming to terms with that specific part of spiritual reality is a key step on the journey to God.

NO GATE AND NO PALACE

Accepting even conditionally, let alone wholeheartedly and without reservation, that God cannot be sought outside the realm of symbol, myth, and metaphor is difficult. But it is also the key to the gate that bars entry to the kingdom of God to most, the single plank of a very narrow bridge across an abyss so wide and so deep that even looking into it is beyond the emotional wherewithal of most people.

Depending on the emotional makeup of the individual attempting to accept it as part of his or her spiritual reality, this idea is going to be either highly invigorating or intensely distressing even to attempt to fathom. It can be ignored, just as can most unpalatable truths. But it cannot be dispensed with or side-stepped forever by any who hope to come to the knowledge of God in the context of unqualified spiritual integrity. For example, it is a basic principle of faith that God exists in a state of such total ubiquity that no place is, or ever could be, totally devoid of the divine and this is the reason the ancients took to calling God "the Place"—because, as Rav Huna taught in the name of Rav Ami, "although the world is not the place of God, God is nevertheless the Place of the World" (B'reishit Rabbah 68:9). Still, most human beings find it impossible to conceive of existence absent at least some sort of physicality and so Jewish authors, even in biblical times, developed the custom of writing and speaking about God as though the Almighty were a celestial king who rules over the world from a magnificent palace in heaven just as the earthly kings of their day ruled over their kingdoms from splendid earthly ones. And, indeed, countless passages in Scripture are developed along this metaphoric range. For example, there is a verse in the Torah in which the pious supplicant calls upon God to "look down from Your holy palace, from heaven, and bless Your people Israel" (Deuteronomy 26:15). I have recited those words hundreds of times in the course of my years on earth. (They constitute part of the prayer that descendants of the priests of ancient times like myself recite after offering the congregation God's trifold blessing.) But coming to terms with what they do and do not—and also cannot—mean is a different story entirely.

Eventually, this kind of language took root so totally that people began to imagine that God actually does dwell in heaven in the manner of an earthly sovereign maintaining a palatial residence in a nation's capital city. As a result, this notion—that God rules the world in the manner of a king ruling his kingdom—became the context in which the faithful found it possible to discuss God without becoming too tangled up in metaphysics for the conversation to be intelligible even to themselves, let alone to ordinary people attempting to learn from their discourse. To say that the concept of King God is untrue is to miss the point, however: although the concept has no real meaning outside of the sphere of poetic mythology, it is not wrong *per se* for people to think of themselves as capable of ascending to the foot of God's heavenly throne through the performance of the commandments. Why would it be? Nor is it wrong or foolish to imagine that each commandment possesses the ability to make the individuals performing it feel that they have brought themselves one step closer toward God's celestial palace in the sky.

The bottom line: there is nothing wrong with thinking about God mythologically *or* poetically ... only in denying that that is what you are doing so.

The journey to faith is not for the fainthearted or the easily discouraged. Yes, it begins with the proverbial single step. But, as is the case with respect to any journey, that single first step only bears real worth when it leads to another ... and that is true even though it is also so that the single steps under consideration have nothing to do with real footsteps, single or multiple, because the journey which they begin is one that takes place outside both of time and space to a God who exists with reference to neither. And accepting this truth is tantamount to passing through the first gate on the journey to the divine palace where God dwells and, surely among other things, waits for the intrepid pilgrim occasionally actually to arrive.

Chapter Two

The Second Gate

Believing in God

People speak all the time about "believing in God" as though the concept were a simple hurdle that anyone possessed of even a modicum of spiritual energy should be able easily to clear with room to spare. Indeed, the whole concept strikes most people as so basic, and so unchallengeable, as almost to be axiomatic. And yet, when pressed to say what the concept itself means *precisely*, most people—including those who answer in the affirmative automatically when asked casually if they believe in God—step immediately back and take refuge either in sarcasm or belligerency. Such people mostly do so *not* because they seriously regard the question as an affront to their dignity or their integrity, however, but because they cannot think of an answer that does not make the alacrity with which they leapt to answer the question sound ridiculous . . . and also because, deep within, they know—and know absolutely—that any response that presents belief in God as a self-evident truth only a true dunce would deny is, almost by definition, a statement interpretable only with reference to the gullibility of the person saying it aloud.

Belief in God is the second gate, the one set in the wall that can be approached only by those who somehow manage, if not to know God, then at the very least to know *of* God in the reasonable, decorous manner of people who believe wholeheartedly in the reality of the world around them. It can take a lifetime to approach this gate. Furthermore, it is perfectly possible to approach it, but never actually to step through it. And yet, for all the gate may appear narrow and tightly shut to most who do manage to approach it, the fact remains that there *are* people who believe in God . . . and whose belief is *not* tainted with arrogance or preening conceit. Therefore, it must be possible to step through this gate into the realm of honest faith.

Taking that first step, however, requires coming to terms with the unsettling truth that believing in God is not really different from believing in anything else. Existing precisely where sensory perception meets an individual's perceived ability to decipher and interpret the world, beliefs are theories that appear never to be disproven by experience . . . and this is so regardless of whether a person does or does not possess the ability to explain the phenomenon in question scientifically. We believe in gravity, therefore, not because we are all physicists or students of physics, but because none of us has ever seen a peach knocked off a table and not fall to the floor. We believe in the sweetness of sugar not because we are all chemists or students of chemistry, but because we have never put a cube of sugar in a cup of coffee and not observed it to make the coffee sweet. But to say that we believe in God not because we are all great theologians or religious philosophers, but because we have *never* failed to notice the beneficent presence of God influencing, guiding, and watching over the men and women with whom we share life on this planet . . . that statement, if it could ever have been said sincerely, certainly cannot be said aloud with conviction in this post-Shoah world by anyone truly sane. And yet faith in God, for all it should fail the test of reasonability peaches or cups of sweet coffee pass effortlessly, is neither impossible nor unattainable.

At its most basic, the search for faith in God is really the search undertaken by would-be believers for perceptible traces of the divine in daily life and there surely *are* people in the world who really have come to find belief in the reality of God no more difficult to sustain than faith in gravity *or* in the sweetness of sugar. However, proclaiming belief in God and actually believing are not the same thing . . . and people who insist that they believe in all sorts of dogmatic beliefs about God that are neither self-evident nor even particularly likely to be true—and which cannot be proven or disproven even inconclusively—merely because they feel obliged to pay lip service to the specific articles of faith in question are not moving in a productive spiritual direction. The Bible was right that "a fool will believe anything" (Proverbs 14:15). But it hardly follows that the wise are therefore to be defined as people who believe in nothing. As always, it comes down to the integrity of the spirit and the intellect. Faith is a reasonable destination, but lying about God does not lead there. Ever.

THE HIGHWAY TO FAITH

To start with the simplest of assertions, people come to belief in God over years and decades by slowly acquiring the building blocks of faith. Stories about faith coming simply and easily as the result of unanticipated and unearned epiphanies are just so much snake oil. There are no short cuts, no quick fixes. No one *just* wakes up one day believing in God. Professing belief is not the same as believing. Feeling obliged to believe is not the same as believing. Acting *as though* you believe is not believing. Even seeing is not believing, not really. In the end, only believing is believing. And belief, like trust, is not acquirable as a commodity you can buy, borrow, or steal. It can only come of its own accord, just as the king's lover in the Song of Songs (and, later, the Supremes) said of love.

If you don't know the supreme Song or can't recall the Supremes' song, I suggest you learn three Hebrew words and take them to heart: *et tzenu·im ḥokhmah*. They come from the Book of Proverbs (11:2) and they mean that wisdom resides (solely) with the humble of spirit, which is to say: with those who divest themselves of arrogance, who refuse to lie about God, who do not imagine there can be any merit in saying they believe things they cannot prove and which therefore could just as easily be false. *Et tzenu·im ḥokhmah.* To be wise in the ways of God, you have to have the courage to own up to the limitations of your human intellect.

In the end, the path toward belief *in* God is paved with specific articles of belief *about* God that the faithful acquire slowly over long years of spiritual effort and enterprise. It isn't that complex a procedure, just an arduous one. And it is the single procedure that religion itself exists to facilitate. The highway to faith originates in the willing intellect and ends in God. The specific *things* we come to believe about God are its paving stones and, as would be the case in any road-building project undertaken by a single individual, they must be set in the earth one at a time. Some are heavy, others light. Some are lovely to look at, others not so much. Some require huge amounts of mortar to hold them in their designated spots, while others appear to fall into place almost of their own accord. Some erode quickly, others only very slowly . . . and still others appear not to erode at all in any significant way even over millennia of use.

And another point is also worth making, this one particularly germane to Judaism: the role of ritual and symbolic rite in religion has nothing to do with personal pleasure or with pageantry, but rather with the effort slowly and steadily to facilitate the inculcation of the specific ideas and principles that serve faith as its inner core of dogmatic support beams and girders. As a result, every single commandment of Scripture may be described as an inner core idea that has been provided with some sort of ritual activity capable of translating it into the world of physicality—and, thus, of granting it the kind of reality ordinary human beings can perceive easily. The ritual side of every commandment is therefore only its outer shell, one capable both of protecting *and* obscuring its inner ideational core just the armor medieval warriors wore both protected them from their enemies' lances *and* hid them from public view. These two aspects—the inner idea and the outer ritual—are always somehow related, but they are never identical. A good model for thinking about this would be the relationship between someone's body and the clothing that obscures that body from public view—the two are obviously going to be related in terms of size and shape, but no rational person could ever confuse the two . . . or doubt their relative worth or ultimate importance. If you tear a shirt and do not wish to pay a tailor to repair it, after all, you can always just put on a different shirt.

The analogy to clothing works in another way as well, actually, in that a garment can reveal a lot or a little depending on the specific kind of fabric from which it was fashioned, the skill-level of the artisan who created it, and how precisely its dimensions match those of the individual wearing it. Similarly, the various rituals commanded by the Torah will reveal either much or little of the ideas that exist at their generative cores depending on the level of dedication, insight, intelligence, and practical halakhic knowledge their performers bring to them. And this is a key concept for the would-be faithful to embrace because all who devote themselves to a ritual without giving any attention to the idea or ideas that that specific ritual exists to bring into the lives of the people performing them—such people have embraced superstition rather than religion. To put the matter in specifically Jewish terms, the whole point of piety is to perform the commandments according to even the most picayune detail of law and custom without losing track of the idea that rests at the core of each commandment undertaken . . . and especially without allowing the elaborate set of strictures in which generations of legal scholars have encased each commandment to obscure the larger goal inherent in the very nature of worship through the medium of law, which is the acceptance of the inner idea by means of the outer ritual.

Scripture says that the ancient Israelites painted the doorposts of their homes in Egypt with the blood of the paschal lamb as a sign that God should pass over their homes and smite instead the homes of their Egyptian tormentors. A *midrash* preserved in the ancient rabbinic commentary on Exodus called the *Mekhilta of Rabbi Ishmael* (Bo §6) adds the fascinating detail, however, that—at least in the opinion of some rabbis—it was not the outside, but the inside of the doors that were daubed with the lamb's blood. The point, after all, was not to tell God which homes were Israelite residences, which detail an omniscient God would surely already have known, but rather for the *ritual* of painting the doorpost to suggest to the enslaved Israelites the *concept* of God as the source of their imminent liberation.

Ultimately, any ritual act that does not bring its performer at least slightly closer to God cannot be considered a real act of worship. Moreover, performing any of the commandments without allowing its ritual to move the performer to embrace the idea that rests at its core is precisely the kind of worship Scripture characterizes as pointless, as in the prophet's oracle in which God commands the people to "bring no more pointless offerings" (Isaiah 1:13). And what could be more pointless than a religious life devoted to the cultivation of rituals that have no ideational base, to the pursuit of form that lacks real content, or to the propagation of halakhic punctiliousness that fails to lead to spiritual advancement?

EMBRACING PARADOX

There is a certain sense in which all religion is built on paradox, but it is the concept of faith in God that rests on the most maddening paradox of them all. On the one hand, belief in God will always remain an elusive goal for those who have not come to feel the presence of the Almighty as the moving force in their lives. On the other, a deep, untroubled sense of God's role in human affairs will come to most as a function of their priorly acquired faith in God. Therefore, in this just like love, faith *ought* to be impossible. Yet, somehow, it remains a real option for thoughtful, non-delusional people. Honesty is key, however: hypocrites tell lies to the gullible, but there is nothing at all hypocritical about devoting a lifetime to unraveling the riddle of faith that is the secret of God's presence in the world of ordinary people.

THE JOURNEY THAT IS ITS OWN DESTINATION

Given God's apparent disinclination to be seen or heard in the simple, uncomplicated way, say, that dogs and birds are seen and heard by regular people out and about in the world, faith untroubled by doubt or worry feels as though it should be sustainable only within the context of a life given over to fantasy or delusion. Or, perhaps even worse, to the kind of mental and spiritual vacuity that risks turning the principles of religion from eternal pillars of iron and steel—pillars upon which a permanent, ongoing relationship with God *can* effectively be built—into pillars of mud and straw upon which no permanent structure could ever be erected, let alone maintained practically, permanently, or successfully.

Nonetheless, faith is possible—when it is defined not as untroubled certainty but as the great (and never quite *fully* attained) goal of a life spent in search of spiritual communion with God. The point is that this state of intense spiritual seeking, called *d'rishat ha-elohim* in Hebrew, is *itself* the final station on a journey toward belief in God that has neither beginning in real space nor end, neither describable itinerary nor chartable trajectory. The journey is thus its own destination. And this is so even despite the fact that God, almost by definition, exists outside the normal framework of time and space that human beings generally find essential to journeys undertaken at all, let alone completed.

Chapter 2

CONTEMPLATING EVIL

To hear people explain that they believe in God, but not in the simple, everyday way they believe in the existence of the lawnmowers in their garden sheds or of the socks on their feet is to hear the voices of people who want to believe and who perhaps even feel a sacred duty to believe, but who don't actually believe in God in the way human beings actually believe in the things in the world they find it impossible to imagine do not exist.

When confronted with this thought, however, most people have a regular set of defenses they utilize to justify the degree to which they have failed to embrace belief in God in the natural, ordinary way they believe in every other thing they feel certain exists. For example, it is regular to hear people explaining—or rather, explaining away—the defects in their faith with reference to the degree to which they are troubled by the existence of brutality, violence, and wickedness in the world. But there is something intensely illogical about that argument: the existence of barbarism and cruelty in the world does not need to lead to a renunciation of normal, simple faith in God any more than the reality of people's faith in God needs logically to require them not to believe in the existence of barbaric, cruel people. Indeed, the very fact that people are able to lead lives devoted, as they see fit, to good *or* to evil means only that the relationship of God to the world is nothing like the relationship of puppeteers to their puppets or, even, of trainers to the dogs they train. Nor would it be any more logical to say that the existence of evil people in the world disproves the existence of God than it would be to say that the existence of evil people disproves the existence of good and merciful people in the world—and this is what the psalmist meant when he looked out at the world and first noted that "the evil are sprouting up like grass" (Psalm 92:8), and then continued in the very next verse with the assertion that, nonetheless, "You are forever exalted, O God" (Psalm 92:9). There are two separate realities, discrete and distinct—something like continuing to believe in the existence of good health even when you yourself are feeling feverish and queasy.

A BRIDGE OF IDEAS

And then there are the generalists, people who are prepared to embrace belief *in* God as long as it does not actually require them to believe in any specific thing *about* God. It sounds attractive—somewhat in the way that it is dramatically easier to fall in love with love itself than with an actual person—but, in the end, attempting to believe in God generically is like trying to speak in "language" without actually speaking in any particular one of the world's languages. And this is so despite the fact that it is seriously easier—and *much* less spiritually stressful—to profess a general sort of undefined belief in God without actually professing any specific thing about God to be true.

It isn't easy, this business of coming to faith in God. Belief in God as the Creator of the world, for example, is anything but simple to accept as unambiguous dogma. Indeed, coming to believe that God made the world—and that, despite the degree to which human beings have spoiled it, the world made by God remains essentially good—seems as though it ought to be beyond anyone familiar with the torments that regularly afflict so many in our world. But although the world itself may well be far too narrow to serve as a bridge to God for the casual wanderer, the commandments are somehow more than strong enough to serve as planks in a bridge of ideas that allow the pilgrim thirsting for intimacy and communion with the divine to cross into the domain of the sacred. And that, we know from empirical, verifiable reality.

The commandments, therefore, may be described both as steppingstones on the path toward faith and as rungs on the ladder reaching up to heaven. They possess the power to transform the world into an arena in which the individual can seek God and come to faith in God without being paralyzed by the woes of the world . . . or by the absurdity of seeking communion with a God whose perceptible reality can only be experienced occasionally and for the most fleeting of unanticipated moments. It is for this reason, in fact, that the way of Torah is not to encourage the faithful to flee from the world and to live as hermits in remote desert hideaways, but rather to live in the world among people and in that setting to sanctify the world and transform it from a place of misery to a place of redemptive potential and potential redemption. The misery of the world will only eliminate the possibility of belief for those unwilling to see in religion the context for addressing that misery with a sacred amalgam of hope, faith, and trust.

RITUAL CAN NEVER BE ITS OWN JUSTIFICATION

Coming to terms with the nature of worship is an absolute prerequisite for coming to believe in God. For instance, although it is true that the commandments, taken as a whole, exist to foster and nourish a general kind of faith in God, it is also the case that each *specific* commandment of the Torah is designed and intended to exercise a *specific* area of faith within the larger context of an individual's set of beliefs. They have no other point. They neither bring good fortune nor, indeed, do they have any effect at all on anyone other than the individual who performs them. (Giving charity to the poor, for example, obviously helps the person receiving the alms financially, but will probably not lead to that individual's spiritual advancement.) The commandments, therefore, are neither guarantors of blessing nor harbingers of redemption, but merely opportunities to make the path to God more accessible by making the twists and turns of that labyrinthine road into a more travelable path than most people would be able to create on their own. That, however, is hardly a reason to disparage them. Just the contrary is true, actually: the ability to make travelable that path is surely one of the greatest of all God's blessings.

The commandments connected with Passover, for example, are all parts of a great picture drawn on the canvas of the world of a God who liberates slaves from bondage and functions as the great source of human freedom in the world. This story found its literary frame in the story of the flight of Israel from Egyptian bondage as told in the Book of Exodus. *Believing* in the historicity of this story, however, is not the point, nor will doing so yield spiritual gain any more than *believing* in the reality of the weights and exercise equipment at the gym will increase your physical strength or stamina. Indeed, just the opposite is the case: those who believe wholeheartedly in the historicity of the biblical account of the exodus from Egypt (*and* who eat *matzah* and bitter herbs on the eve of Passover *and* in whose homes not even a molecule of leavened bread or cake is to be found for the entire length of the festival), but who are not propelled by their efforts any closer than they previously were toward accepting the notion that God can function in their own lives as the source of freedom and liberation—such people cannot be said to have come any closer to real faith through the performance of all those commandments. It is *never* the case that the point of performing a commandment is that that commandment be performed. In matters of faith, just as in love, rituals can never serve as their own justification.

There was once a rabbi who started a huge brouhaha by suggesting that the story of the Exodus might not be historically accurate in its every detail. Whether he regrets his remarks now or not, I have no idea. But watching the whole tempest unfold was instructive in its own right: there were people who wanted these stories to be true and who were prepared to go to the mat to argue for their absolute historicity as though there were any real importance to the concept. And they were prepared to do so despite the obvious fact that at least some details recorded in Scripture cannot possibly be true. For instance, let's consider the detail Scripture reports to the effect that Pharaoh's daughter gave Moses a Hebrew name based on her Hebrew-language declaration that she had drawn him out of the river. First of all, she didn't draw him out of the river—the text (at Exodus 2:5) specifically says that she sent one of her handmaidens to do that. But more to the point is to ask if it is even remotely plausible that Pharaoh's daughter spoke Hebrew at all, let alone that she could possibly have known it well enough to engage in sophisticated Hebrew word play. Who would have taught it to her? And why? And even if she somehow had learned Hebrew, why wouldn't she have given her adopted son an Egyptian name? And to whom would she have spoken this theoretical

Hebrew of hers anyway—surely not to her Egyptian servants! (Mind you, the Bible depicts Pharaoh as speaking Hebrew too, which seems even less likely!) So that part of the story sounds, at best, highly unlikely to be historically accurate precisely as told . . . and since there is no proof to the contrary, why believe it? Of course, it could be true. So could countless other unlikely details that lend color and texture to that story, yet at least some people felt almost honor-bound to defend the biblical text itself against the aggression of a rabbi whose sole crime was reading carefully and wondering aloud about its detail.

The ensuing battle, however, was a pointless fracas over nothing at all because, in the end, the sole worth of any Bible story lies in the spiritual lesson it teaches or wishes to teach, a point so crucial to a reasonable reading of Scripture that failing to identify and then successfully to internalize the specific lesson at the core of any biblical passage really is to miss the point entirely. Nevertheless, I fully agree that it would be far easier to accept some unlikely detail in a famous story as fact than to believe, let alone wholeheartedly, that you are personally being held back in life by your own failure to find in God the source of your potential liberation from the negative character traits and moral flaws that impede your progress!

TRAVELING SOLO

In the end, the journey toward belief in God is a trip you take on your own. Numbers don't count. Company doesn't matter. Affiliation with a faith community is helpful because it provides encouragement and support to the individual journeyer, not because it makes it any less necessary for every single wanderer in the wilderness to travel down a private road to a personal Jerusalem as a solitary supplicant seeking succor and salvation in God. But the cardinal principle here is that individual pilgrims arrive at the gates of Jerusalem on their own even if they are in the company on that very same road of countless others making the same pilgrimage to the same Temple. Nor is the potential for success in arriving at the gates of the Holy City tied to the number of other people seeking communion with the same God in the same place at the same time. Speaking logically, how could there be? Nor, needless to say, can that number, great or small, be imagined to have any positive or negative impact or influence on God. Indeed, when the prophet, seized by the spirit of prophecy, declared in God's name, "I am God; I do not change" (Malachi 3:6), he meant precisely that: that the existence of God is not predicated—and could not *ever* be predicated—on the piety of the world.

STRENGTH

Although it is certainly so that the reality of divine existence cannot be imagined to depend on the degree to which a given generation embraces faith in God, it is also so that the degree to which faith in the existence of God becomes a factor in human history *inevitably* rises and falls from generation to generation in direct proportion to the degree to which the men and women of that day allow their belief in God to influence their daily actions and activities.

Indeed, to imagine that acclaiming God as the Author of History means believing that the Almighty decides in advance what is going to happen in the world and then organizes things so that everything that is foreordained actually occurs—that image of God as a beneficent puppeteer is nothing more than a pathetic effort to deny the awful truth that the only force in the world that guides history is the will of human beings to conduct themselves in sync with the will of God or not to conduct themselves in that way. To blame God because some particular event did or did not occur, therefore, has to be considered tantamount to the rejection of traditional faith—because blaming God for history requires that the blamers abandon belief in an all-powerful God able to grant human beings absolute control over their behavior in the world.

GOD OF/IN HISTORY

Let's stay with the idea of faith in God being accessible through the contemplation of God's relationship to human history. Although the level of God's apparent involvement with the daily affairs of the world will inevitably vary from era to era directly with the degree to which the men and women of a given generation are prepared to walk in God's ways, it is still illogical—in the total absence of proof—to suppose that an all-powerful God would somehow be unable to act in human history at all. Indeed, Rabbi Akiba's famous paradox—that *although* logic dictates that everything must somehow be foreseen by all-knowing God, human beings are *nevertheless* endowed with the capacity to choose between good and evil—is only another way of saying that God inevitably grants permission to people to conduct themselves in the world in accordance with the just or unjust promptings of their own hearts. (Rabbi Akiba's paradox is preserved in the Mishnah at M. Avot 3:19.) Indeed, it stands to reason that if human beings are able at will to behave as their moral consciences dictate, then this ability must certainly also inhere in the God whom Scripture acclaims as the Author of History. Indeed, arguing that God *cannot* choose to act a specific way within the context of human history would be tantamount to denying the omnipotence of God.

FAITH AND CATASTROPHE

For moderns (and surely not only for modern Jews), it is inconceivable for the road to faith in God not to pass at some point through the gates of Auschwitz. And accepting that, upsetting and disorienting a thought though it may be, is key: there is no point, nor will there even again be a point, in talking about either the omniscience or the omnipotence of God without reference to the Shoah. Indeed, it would be reasonable to say that anyone possessed of a feeling heart and of eyes that see who can look at pictures of crematoria and execution ditches while maintaining—or claiming to maintain—untroubled faith in a benevolent and beneficent God is living, to say the very least, in a world of delusory fantasy.

Countless books and essays on the topic have been published since the truth about the extent of the debacle first became known in the years following the end of the Second World War. Most, perhaps even all, of these efforts were heartfelt and sincere. Yet most are unsatisfying and illogical. The argument, for example, that there is no real problem here because, after all, two-thirds of the world's Jews did *not* die at the hands of the foe—and, moreover, that this detail proves the mercy and compassion of God toward the Jewish people—feels impossible to take seriously. Yet I have heard just that argument put forward several times, including once by someone wearing *t'fillin* while he spoke.

In the final analysis, no one can claim to believe in a God who is the Author of History without attempting to explain how the Shoah fits into that thought. Any who reject the possibility of a solution and argue that embracing faith in God in the post-Shoah era simply requires the would-be believer to look away from Treblinka are in essence arguing that faith in our day is only really available to people who shut their eyes to reality and stop up their ears to keep from hearing anything inconsonant with traditional belief. No one possessed of true spiritual integrity would make that argument, of course. But thinking of an alternative that does not require lying about God—*that* is the challenge laid by history at the feet of any who would serve God in the post-Holocaust world.

DELIGHT AND FRAILTY

The bottom line is that the key to finding faith in God is to be both honest and humble: for all it might be painful to encounter challenges to the simple faith most of us wish we could possess, it is nevertheless possible to feel grateful and beholden for every step toward God that we do take in the context of absolute honesty and an unyielding commitment to spiritual integrity, even if the specific *thing* that inspired us to attain a new level of faith is essentially negative. Indeed, when the psalmist wrote, "I delight in suffering for the sake of learning Your laws / yea, the *torah* of Your mouth is worth more to me than thousands of coins of gold and silver" (Psalm 119:71–72), what I take that to mean is that the poet did not regret all the unhappiness he was obliged to encounter in his life precisely because that misery inspired him to cling all the more closely to the commandments and to devote himself to mastering the minutiae of their proper observance, thereby bringing him through the medium of personal despair and distress to a level of faith in God that he might otherwise never have attained.

Later, this was expressed in the Mishnah with the simple rule requiring that "one bless God no less fervently when bad things happen as when good things do" (M. Berakhot 9:5), the assumption always being that bad happenstances are just as able as more positive events or incidents to bring an individual to faith. The Psalter, more than any other book of the Bible, is filled to overflowing with the idea that sadness, sickness, fear, misery, grief, melancholy, and disappointment are not enemies of faith, but can serve as its wellsprings. The fact that it is precisely in times of distress and worry that the human spirit comes most easily to faith is not a sign of lunacy, merely of sensitivity.

There are as many roads to Jerusalem as there are pilgrims making their slow, sometimes painful, progress along them. Many find the experience joyful and so respond to their own progress with delight. But it has been my personal experience that most people feel the presence of God more keenly at funerals than at weddings, which is precisely what King Kohelet meant all those years ago when he wrote that "the wise are happiest in houses of mourning, whereas fools have more fun at parties (Kohelet 7:4). Dour, cranky words, to be sure. But that only makes them unpalatable and upsetting, not untrue!

Chapter Three

The Third Gate

Reading God

In a sense, the greatest gift the authors of the Hebrew Bible gave to the world is the notion that language itself can become the context in which human beings and God may meet in some sort of swirling vortex of communicative consciousness, creative will, active intelligence, and (mostly) scrutable symbolism. The ancient stuff of that gift, the text of the Hebrew Bible, is thus the platform on which we moderns will do well to stand if we wish to pursue the goal of content-rich spiritual development without having first to reinvent the wheel. (This is not at all the same as saying that you *may* not reinvent the wheel, just that you don't have to. But if you don't wish to reinvent the wheel, what choice do you have other than to use a wheel someone else has already invented? I suppose you could just walk. But some destinations really are too far away to reach on foot even in the course of a lifetime.)

In my life as a rabbi, I occasionally hear this thought expressed with a kind of underlying resentment, almost as though it somehow demeans an individual's personal journey to faith in God for Western spirituality to have a recorded history. That argument lacks cogency, but even if that weren't the case, making a virtue out of ignoring the past would still almost always be a prideful error rooted more in egotism than in practicality. As a result, interpreting an individual's personal refusal to acknowledge the role of Scripture in the history of human spirituality as a sign of intellectual independence will almost always be as fruitless an endeavor as attempting to gain a profound understanding of anything at all by making a virtue of proudly ignoring the context in which others have pursued the same goal and the specific ways in which they were or weren't successful.

For better or for worse, and with all the maddening inconsistencies of theology and anthropology it presents *and* the relentless obscurity of so many of its passages (including some of its most famous ones) *and* the way so many of its tales confront Western morality at all its weakest points, the text of the Bible is *still* the bedrock upon which the spiritual enterprise will rest for most of us as we make our way forward through the night toward the light of God's presence.

For both Jews and Christians eager to be propelled forward along their personal paths to spiritual fulfillment by the flow of history, therefore, the pursuit of God will inevitably involve the need to confront the text of the Hebrew Bible. Yet, for all it sounds as though it should be a simple task, there actually *is* no more difficult task than reading the Bible without succumbing to the siren call of self-righteous delusion. Reading the book honestly and openly, taking words and phrases in their historical and literary contexts, refusing to impute indefensible interpretations to words just because doing so would appear to substantiate some unrelated piece of dogma—all of these are basic norms of reading that any normal reader would bring to any book worth studying with care. Yet these basic principles are features of only the rarest work of biblical research undertaken outside the realm of pure scholarship . . . and there are books among the best-selling and most widely read works of modern spiritual literature that proudly trumpet their authors' disinclination to adopt *any* of them at all . . . and which make a virtue, albeit a perverse one, out of those authors' proud refusal to encounter the text of Scripture in the forthright and honest way that they would naturally bring to any other book in the world that they might come across and read.

How exactly to read the Bible is one of the great challenges that faces anyone who would seek God in the framework of Judaism *or* Christianity. (Whether Islam could or should be included in that thought is an interesting question best left for Muslim clerics to debate. But that the Quran itself presumes a working knowledge of the Hebrew Bible goes without saying.) Nonetheless, religious fanaticism in Western culture is generally so allied to scriptural fundamentalism that it is actually unusual to find a true Jewish or Christian religious fanatic who is not also a fundamentalist with respect to the text of Scripture. The reason Bible-thumpers thump Bibles is part of this same reality: the *bona fides* of any true religious conservative in our society appears to rest most securely in that individual's willingness to assert total and unquestioning faith in the divine nature of the biblical text and in the unerring moral worth of its every lesson. Lack of scientific evidence for any specific claim about the text is not considered a crucial or even a substantial problem. Indeed, the relatively tame suggestion that faith in the worth of Scripture should be rooted in an intellectually defensible assessment of the developmental history of its text is capable of arousing almost combative anger in some circles—including some whose members really should know better.

Nevertheless, it is well worth noting that no amount of bluster can actually change the nature of the biblical text or affect its worth for those who would seek God in the context of unwavering fidelity to their own spiritual heritage or their own spiritual integrity.

THE TRIPLE PRISM

And so we begin with a single incontrovertible principle: that, for all we might wish otherwise to be the case, we have neither conclusive nor even especially convincing circumstantial evidence that even a single letter of the text of the Bible was written by God in the uncomplicated manner of mortal authors sitting down at their writing desks to write a book or compose an essay. For all this idea might be upsetting and disorienting to some, though, the most defensible way to conceptualize the situation is to suppose—realistically and plausibly—that the written text of Scripture is the experience of God's presence as focused through the triple alembic of human perceptive consciousness, prophetic literary creativity, and, yes, the incredible hubris of human beings who dare imagine that the ineffable can be expressed at all in one of their made-up languages. I am well aware that many will disagree—but surely the burden of proof must rest on the shoulders of any who claim that God wrote the Torah and then handed it over to Moses in the simple, wholly noncomplex manner of an individual writing a word on a slip of paper and then handing it to the person standing next to him. The endless harping of fundamentalists on the topic notwithstanding, however, even *unconvincing* arguments in favor of such a literalist approach to Scripture have yet to be adduced.

The path to God can never be paved with lies or half-truths. Speaking of those who will survive the upheavals that life brings to more or less all and *still* remain wholehearted members of the House of Israel, an ancient prophet wrote, "The remnant of Israel will neither act sinfully nor speak lies" (Zephaniah 3:13) and his words remain as trenchant and challenging as they must have been when first spoken aloud. Details concerning the specific context in which those words actually *were* first spoken aloud are now long lost, of course. That really is too bad, but the message for latter-day devotees of Bible-based religions inherent in those words—that no attempt to know God through the medium of Bible study will ever succeed through the promulgation of fantasies or falsehoods about the history or basic nature of the sacred text, and that this is so no matter how convenient it would be for otherwise to be the case—that deeply monitory message remains today as profoundly important as ever for all who seek to advance spiritually unimpeded by roadblocks erected by themselves on the paths forward they are at the same time attempting to follow.

THE YOKE OF TRUTH

Fundamentalists like to argue against taking a scientific approach to the nature, history, and holiness of the books of Scripture on the practical grounds that taking such an approach will inevitably make it impossible to approach the biblical text seriously or fully respectfully. In my experience, however, just the contrary is far more likely to be the case: seeking the God of truth along a path of wishful thinking and wistful half-truths is far less likely to lead to real spiritual gain than pursuing the very same set of spiritual goals in the context of an unyielding commitment to absolute honesty and an unwavering sense of intellectual integrity. The right to wander the path forward to profound spiritual growth laid down in Scripture must be a result of a lifetime devoted to wholly honest thinking about the texts that propose that program to would-be pilgrims seeking to set out on the road to Jerusalem and should not be based—and perhaps even *cannot* be based—on of fanciful notions about their origins that, at least in the end, will be discarded by all but the most irremediably gullible.

The high road that leads to communion with God begins where the intellect and the heart meet in the context of guileless readiness to move forward unencumbered by fantasy and falsehood, and can best be conceptualized as a journey that begins wherever you are when you set out and continues on toward the place in which God has chosen to settle the divine name, toward Jerusalem. But only those whom the poet calls "those who call out to God in truth" (Psalm 145:18) may wander this path and this, in turn, is what the author of the 119th psalm meant with the simple declaration: "I have sought You with all my heart / do not, therefore, allow me to err in the performance of Your commandments" (Psalm 119:10). I suppose the psalmist could have been thinking of any number of different ways we could err in the context of worshipful acts, but how could we do so more grievously than by lying about them and about the nature of the sacred books that recommend them to us? Coming to know the God of truth requires submitting totally, absolutely and unreservedly to the yoke of truth . . . and that precludes lying about God *and* about the nature of the biblical text.

FUNDAMENTALISM

Even people who claim that the holiness of the books of the Bible derives directly from the fact that their origin is to be located within the essential, inner creativity of Author God (and not from the fact that they constitute the endlessly interesting record of their authors' journeys toward God, the source of holiness in the world)—even such people are not obliged by reason or logic to believe that the biblical text embodies the perfect, uncorrupted word of God as magically transmitted from generation to generation without even the slightest orthographical or scribal error ever having crept in here and there. They may well be guilty more of naiveté about the scribal arts than wickedness, but that naiveté morphs into hypocrisy when, *after* proclaiming their absolute faith in the inviolate nature of the biblical text, such people *then* flinch when they find texts within the biblical corpus that speak approvingly of chattel slavery, bigamy and polygamy, the sexual abuse of female prisoners-of-war, and the genocidal slaughter of an enemy nation's infants. Indeed, by declining to accept these institutions and concepts as integral, wholly acceptable parts of their spiritual worldview, such people are betraying their own alleged commitment to the divine authority of Scripture. The absolute inerrancy of Scripture is a notion that cannot be embraced selectively.

And this as well: people who attempt to justify their biblical fundamentalism by insisting that certain specific passages in the Torah belong to a special class of rules and regulations that are no longer operative (as opposed to others that have eternal, unvoidable validity), but who are unable to explain in simple language how precisely they know which passages belong to which category, such people are *also* guilty of taking the name of God in vain. In the end, their approach to the biblical text sounds sincere and might even *be* sincere, but their claims actually trivialize both the sanctity of the divine text *and* the challenge it lays down to moderns who would approach God along its labyrinthine literary byways.

THE LONELY ROAD

Delusional fantasies, even when honestly embraced, will lead neither to intellectual clarity nor to spiritual growth. The notion, for example, that the study of Scripture will inevitably lead to faith in God—and then, either inevitably or at least ideally, to a state of ongoing communion with the divine realm—is a fantasy that derives directly from the peculiar notion that the Bible is a kind of screen that separates heaven and earth, and that studying its text is a way—not speaking metaphorically or symbolically, but plainly and simply— that studying its text is a way of piercing through this barrier for the sake of undertaking a journey to the heavenly palace in which Sovereign God sits and waits patiently for the faithful few finally to arrive. On the other hand, forgetting—even briefly—that all humanly conceived images of God are necessarily metaphors and symbols is the ultimate blasphemy. The bottom line is that the text of Scripture is not some incredibly complicated puzzle that will automatically usher those happy few who solve it correctly into the heavenly throne room, but rather a lit torch that has the special ability to illumine the lonely road that pilgrims spend a lifetime attempting to follow to the saving presence of God.

HEARING GOD

Spiritual integrity is not wisely confused with cynicism. The prophets, for example, appear to have been the real thing: men and women possessed of the *uncanny*, in some cases even perhaps the *unexpected*, ability to focus an indelible impression of God's communicative presence through the prism of their own articulacy. We can assert that *not* because we *know* it to be the case—which would be impossible to state categorically and with absolute certainty so many centuries after the fact—but because it strikes us that way . . . and therefore we may certainly say just that: that the prophets appear to us to have felt themselves to be genuine messengers of God, not charlatans or tricksters playing out a role for the sake of personal gain or self-aggrandizement. However, at the same time we say that, we must also accept—and accept wholeheartedly and without any inner reservation—that, in the absence of clear, unequivocal scientific evidence, it is impossible to state with certainty if a specific prophetic oracle has its origins within God or within the inner spiritual consciousness of the prophet in whose name or in whose book it is recorded in Scripture. Either is possible. Nor is it necessarily the case that the prophets *themselves* could always, or ever, distinguish easily between the two. The issue of spiritual integrity doesn't come into play in terms of knowing which is the correct interpretation of any specific oracle, which information has to be considered unknowable. However, it does come into play in terms of *knowing* that knowing which interpretation is correct is an impossibility and being willing to move on from there.

The difference between people who harbor a sense of God's ongoing presence in their lives, yet who do *not* speak words of prophecy, and those who have that same sense of God's perceptible reality but somehow *are* able to speak in the name of God has to do with different people naturally possessing different levels of creative talent, linguistic expressivity, and spiritual openness. Different people, of course, will inevitably feel themselves called to respond to the sense of God's presence in their lives in different ways. And the unwillingness, or even the inability, of some to translate that specific experience into human language is also part of the larger picture. What the difference between prophetic types and lay people most definitely does not—and also cannot—reflect, however, is the spurious assertion that there are different, magically pre-assigned, levels of human ability to hear the voice of God, an ability that reason dictates all human beings created by the same God must share equally. The analogy to music is apt: all hearing people can hear music, but only very few can successfully take melodies that they alone hear in their heads and use them to create music that others can hear and enjoy. And fewer still can do so in a way that speaks universally to listeners from diverse cultures and epochs.

This is the truth to which the prophet Amos alluded when he asked aloud "When Adonai-Elohim (that is: the Lord God) speaks, who will *not* prophesy?" (Amos 3:8), which can only mean that the prophet found it impossible to imagine that the gift of prophecy could be granted solely to some of God's children and not to others. And it is also the truth hiding behind the wishful outburst of Moses recorded in the Book of Numbers: "Would that all of God's people were prophets!" (Numbers 11:29), which words would make no sense at all if the people were not all at least *theoretically* capable of hearing the voice of God.

BOOK, NOT MACHINE

The word of God is a hammer that that can be used to build or to destroy, to construct or to destruct. Indeed, the fact that Scripture can be a tool or a weapon is what the prophet intended us to understand when he spoke in the name of God and proclaimed that the word of God is "like fire . . . *and* like a hammer capable of smashing rock" (Jeremiah 23:29)—that is to say, divine speech is like a tool in someone's hand that itself is neither good nor bad, but which can be used for good or for bad by the individual in question. But, for all the elemental spuriousness that inheres naturally in any individual's effort to seek God according to someone else's playbook, there is nevertheless no straighter path toward communion with God than the principled, thoughtful study of Scripture.

Unfortunately, there is also no more crooked path an individual might walk without ever coming anywhere near the goal of attaining communion with God than the study of Scripture. It's a bit of a paradox, admittedly, but this is how things are and, indeed, the Bible can be a permanently flowing fountain of religious strength and creative tension in the hands of the humble of spirit and the modest of temperament because it really is so that "wisdom abides with the humble" (Proverbs 11:2). In hands of the arrogant and the insolent who insist that the Bible is whatever they wish and then proclaim it to be, on the other hand, there can be no greater roadblock to spiritual growth than the obfuscatory veneration of the biblical text. As a result, the biblical text has the capacity to serve as the gateway to heaven through which guileless pilgrims may surely pass on their way to the knowledge of God, but *also* as an impenetrable barrier between the world and its Creator when approached with presumptuousness rooted in the arrogant fantasy that an ancient text can have whatever meaning someone living thousands of years later wishes it to have.

OBEDIENCE AND REDEMPTION

There is the Torah that rests in the Holy Ark of any synagogue—and "this is the Torah that Moses set before the children of Israel" (Deuteronomy 4:44)—but there is also another Torah, the one written neither on parchment nor with ink—and with neither words nor letters of any sort—yet in which is nevertheless written all that human beings know or may ever know of God. Written without writing, this Torah consists solely of desire and longing for God, and it is the book written in what Scripture calls the language of truth, soundless speech so potent that even "the deaf can hear the words of a book" (Isaiah 29:18) written in it.

In turn, the commandments of the Torah reflect the dual nature of their parent text: there are outer, physical aspects to each commandment, but also deeply interior aspects as well . . . and these latter aspects are the ones that are about neither the way the faithful eat nor the way they conduct their affairs, but rather the way they succeed or fail at living out the days of their years in the shadow of God's abiding presence on earth. In the end, the ultimate worth of any worshipful act rests in its ability to bring an individual to a moment of pure, unadulterated longing for God and then, in the course of a lifetime spent in pursuit of such moments, to move that person onto the road to Jerusalem. In this way, a commandment can reasonably and rationally be acclaimed as a holy act that brings those who cleave unto it to the source of holiness in the world, the God acclaimed in Scripture as the Holy One of Israel. In the hands of those who merely see the commandments as bargaining chips in a lifelong effort to get God to do this or that thing, however, those same commandments become rituals devoid of true spiritual power—except for the power to distance those who cling to them from the very God into whose elusive presence they claim so ardently to wish to enter.

DISCERNING CONSCIOUSNESS

The world is full to overflowing with people who are prepared to devote themselves wholly to the study of sacred texts on the sole condition that they are never required, or even expected, actually to learn anything that might possibly confuse or upset them, or force them to reevaluate—and perhaps even slightly to change, let alone radically to alter—their religious beliefs and opinions. Their devotion is intense, but the bottom line is still that the study of the Bible—or of any religious text—is only meaningful when the act of learning serves as a way of seeking God's presence between the lines of a text under consideration. Moreover, study that is not characterized by intellectual probity and spiritual integrity cannot be considered a worshipful act at all because it cannot create a reasonable context for seeking God through the medium of the discerning intellect.

In the end, the study of Scripture becomes a worshipful act when the act of self-immersion in a text creates a path that leads from a student's own starting point, wherever that may be, to the great goal of ongoing, content-rich communion with the Holy One of Israel. Unfortunately, study can also be an exercise in pretentiousness and self-puffery that creates an almost impenetrable barrier between students whose interest in the word of God does not extend beyond the justification of their own prior beliefs and the God whom they claim to wish to serve through the study of sacred texts.

EATING A PEACH

The famous—and well beloved—distinction between traditional exegesis and the scientific study of the biblical text does and doesn't exist.

It exists in the sense that the scientific scholar is generally interested in the history of the text and so attempts to uncover the precise set of literary and historical processes that transformed the text from its earliest version into the precise text that has come down into our hands as part of Scripture. The traditional exegete, on the other hand, is generally far more interested in the text as it actually exists in our day and is more focused, therefore, on attempting to discover the various layers of subcutaneous meaning that rest just beneath its literary surface.

In what sense does it not exist? It does not exist in the sense that the traditional exegete and the modern text scholar share a common end-goal: to encounter the author of a written word through the contemplation of that word. Among the various chapters of Scripture are chapters that were written as simple literary units by single authors for distinct and easily recognizable literary ends. There are, however, also biblical chapters the literary histories of which appear to reflect complex and complicated editorial processes spread out over centuries of development. Still, when even the world's most sophisticated botanist eats a peach, the satisfaction and pleasure that accrue from the experience derive from the flavor and texture of the fruit, not from even the deepest, most impressive knowledge of science. And pathetic indeed would be the scientist rendered incapable of enjoying a cold, juicy peach on a hot summer's day by knowing too much of botany and its endless intricacies simply to enjoy the experience.

Chapter 3

THE USE AND ABUSE OF SCRIPTURE

The whole *concept* of stepping across a bridge of words to God bears some thinking about.

From the religious point of view, a successful student of Scripture is someone who devotes time and energy to the study of the biblical text and, in so doing, comes closer than other students of that same text to the original intent of its author. Dramatically less praiseworthy, however, are those who devote time and energy to the study of biblical texts merely in order to justify some previously held opinion or to buttress one or another conviction they consider essential or indispensable to their worldview. (The efforts of people in this second category will always come to naught *not* because they will inevitably fail to think up some interesting interpretation of the text in question, but rather in the sense that textual study undertaken in the context of foregone conclusion cannot be considered study at all.) But least praiseworthy of all are those who purport to be students of Scripture, but who approach ancient texts without displaying any real interest at all in communing with their authors through the medium of those authors' written words or even, in the extreme case, without being willing to admit that the texts they are considering actually *had* human authors at all.

TRANSLATING HEBREW

Is the fact that the Bible is not written in "language" itself or, impossibly, in *every* language, but in a specific language—Hebrew with a bit of Aramaic thrown in here and there—just a detail based on the fact that all spoken or written words by their nature have to be spoken or written in a some specific language from among the languages of humankind? Or is there some specific importance to the fact that the words of the Bible were bequeathed by their framers to the generations to follow in Hebrew? Does that merely reflect the fact that *those* people spoke *that* language? Or is there some other point? And, if so, whatever could it be?

At first, the whole question sounds a bit silly even to ask out loud. Shakespeare wrote in English because that was the language he spoke. Goethe wrote in German for the same reason, as did Tolstoy in Russian. It is self-evident, then, that *those* authors did not choose their languages from all the languages of the world, but rather were limited by their own cultural milieus—and by the natural wish that the people with whom they shared those cultural milieus be able to read their works. But is the same true for the authors of the texts we know collectively as the Bible? They also lived in a specific cultural milieu and spoke a specific language, after all. Is the Hebrew of Scripture merely a function of cultural happenstance? Surely, after all, the prophets of old Jerusalem didn't have the option of delivering their oracles in Korean or Gaelic!

And yet, for all the language of Scripture surely *must* be taken as a function of the cultural milieu in which its framers and redactors lived, there is also something remarkable in the way the *specific* nature of the Hebrew language reflects the contents of its most famous book. And, indeed, the holiness of the holy tongue is uncannily reflected in its endless chains of words linked to each other by virtue of common three-letter roots. In turn, these roots, unpronounceable on their own yet fully present in almost every word, make of most words in the language something suggestive of the nature of God's presence in the world in that every Hebrew word exists with and without boundaries, bearing theoretical but ultimately inexpressible meaning until garbed in the sounds and syllables that make the word audible at the same time they interiorize to the point of imperceptibility the unvoiced triliteral root within. Therefore, although the meaning of Hebrew words can be given in other languages, the holiness of the Hebrew tongue—by which I mean to denote the *specific* way in which the language of Scripture mirrors its most fundamental concepts—cannot be translated. As a result, the best success for which translators of the Bible may hope is the accomplishment of conveying the information contained in a given Hebrew sentence in some other tongue.

Yes, of course the text of the Hebrew Bible was bequeathed to the world in that specific language because that was the language its framers spoke. But it is also so that the *specific* language of the book allows something of the Revealer subtly to be revealed in the revelation. To be content with reading the Bible in translation is therefore to settle. Yet the world is full of such people, almost none of whom would have much—or any—respect for a Shakespearean scholar capable only of reading the bard's plays in translation and not in the language in which they were composed and first performed.

GULLIBILITY AND HUMILITY

Indispensable for any who would pass through the third gateway on the great journey to God will be the ability to distinguish between gullibility and humility.

Being gullible means believing anything anyone tells you regardless of how unlikely it might sound. Being humble, at least in terms of reading Scripture, means accepting—and accepting wholeheartedly and *not* begrudgingly—that there is no such thing—that there *cannot* be such a thing—as a literary composition that deals totally honestly with the nature of God from the vantage point of a particular human author. And it means as well that there is no real meaning to the conclusion that a specific passage in Scripture about the nature of God is right or wrong . . . and that this is true to the extent that discrepancies between two contradictory passages can never be resolved merely by researching the matter to determine which text is the "correct" one. For example, the more useful way to deal with the fact that a famous passage in Exodus decrees that the paschal offering must be chosen from "unblemished male yearlings among the lambs and goats" (Exodus 12:5) and the fact that a parallel passage in the sixteenth chapter of Deuteronomy (16:2) specifically mentions calves as potential offerings is not to decide which law is "correct" from a legal standpoint, or even to spend time attempting to determine which passage accurately reflects the practice in ancient Jerusalem, but rather to suppose that we have before us two slightly different ancient attempts to translate the idea of God as the source of redemption and liberation in the world from the realm of spiritual theorizing into the world of symbolic action.

The specific reason that two versions of the same idea developed along slightly different lines is interesting to ponder, but ultimately unimportant for moderns seeking to know God as the source of liberation in their personal lives through the medium of scriptural study *or* through the medium of Passover observance. Curious people may, of course, legitimately wonder what options the ancients actually did have when it came time each year to choose an animal for the paschal sacrifice. Regretfully, however, the answer has to be that we moderns have no proof one way or the other because the Temple archives that could easily resolve the matter did not survive antiquity. One possibility is that the different texts reflect different historical periods. (This is the approach of most university-based text scholars.) Or perhaps one of the texts simply means something other than what it appears on the surface to mean. (This was the approach of the rabbis of ancient times.) Even if we did have a way of finding a definitive way to resolve the discrepancy, however, it would be interesting solely from a historical point. For men and women of faith seeking to find in God the source of their own potential redemptive liberation from the chains that bind, however, it would not be all that important at all.

DEAD MEN (AND WOMEN) TALKING

Since every effort to explicate a scriptural story is, in effect, a kind of dialogue-out-of-time between a living commentator and a dead story teller, it is inevitable that the prejudices and prior beliefs of commentators about their late partners in dialogue—beliefs including, but not limited to, the genders of those authors, the centuries in which they lived, their political opinions, and the specifics regarding their places in the world in which they lived, worked and flourished—will inevitably affect the quality and nature of those commentators' exegetical work.

One foundational idea that needs to underlie any attempt to seek a palpable sense of the presence of God in the world through the study of Scripture is the principle that the words in a given biblical story may be deemed solely to represent the opinions and beliefs of the author of that story. (In any other literary context, this would seem so obvious as hardly to require saying out loud.) But those opinions and beliefs, frozen as they are within the biblical text, are unable to respond to questions put to them about their authors or even about their own subject matter, which truth is unaffected by the fact that the words of a given biblical text surely *were* composed at a specific moment in history by an actual human being who undoubtedly *did* have a specific identity and hold a specific set of opinions. It follows from this that commentators may speak only on their own behalf and in their own names . . . and never on behalf of the authors of the biblical texts they explicate and certainly never in the names of those authors. Readers more than capable of saying what the text means *to them* must therefore hold back always from declaring what a text meant to its author other than tentatively and hypothetically. That too sounds like a commonplace idea, but the world is full to overflowing with people who feel wholly able to say deep, meaningful things about authors whom they not only haven't ever met but whose names they don't know and regarding the most basic details of whose lives they have no idea at all.

WORDS ARE NOT PEOPLE

And this as well: words, even sacred words, are not people. Therefore, any who immerse themselves in the stories of Scripture are forbidden by reason to deny the historical existence of the authors of the texts they are studying and, even more weirdly, to relate to the literary personalities who appear in those stories as though they themselves were the flesh-and-blood people with whom communion is possible by means of thoughtful literary analysis.

The first hurdle to clear is never to speak of the books of the Bible as though they were people. Thoughtful readers, therefore, do not ask what "Genesis is trying to teach us" in a given passage or why Proverbs "says" whatever it appears to say in a given verse. Being a book, Genesis cannot try to do anything at all, nor can the Book of Proverbs say a word. Instead, readers imbued with a sense of intellectual integrity will always want to recall that every book of the Bible, regardless of its editorial pre-history, exists as a work that was either written from scratch by an author at a given time in history or else was redacted into its present shape and format by an editor working with some anterior work or works. No one seems to have any difficulty keeping Shakespeare and Shylock straight in their minds—or remembering which one was the living person and which the literary character. That, of course, is as it should be. But why then are so many authors unwilling to apply this concept to the various books of Scripture as well?

Texts that purport to be divine oracles are in this category as well: some of the ancient prophets were better than others in translating their experience of the living God into understandable oracular texts, but all the texts bequeathed to us by the prophets of old were written down by someone—either by the prophet personally or by an amanuensis or someone from a later generation who collected the texts that today constitute that prophet's written legacy—and it is with that specific someone that the text offers latter-day readers the possibility of intellectual communion through the medium of the written word.

As a result, it is possible to say that the text of the Bible serves readers as a kind of barrier made of darkened—but not *entirely* opaque—glass that separates the authors of its chapters from modern readers, readers who may surely attempt to commune with the great authors of biblical antiquity as they seek God in their own lives, but who can only practically do so by addressing themselves to the literary characters that appear in those authors' stories . . . characters who exist in our world solely as literary figures in told tales even if men and women with the same names actually *did* live as flesh-and-blood human beings in the day of the authors of those tales, or not in their day. Accepting this doesn't require believing that there wasn't a Queen Esther or a King Solomon in ancient times, only that we can only know them through the sole medium in which their names and deeds were preserved and bequeathed to us.

WORTHLESSNESS AND HISTORICITY

There is a whole literary subcategory devoted to the "But Did It Really Happen?" school of biblical scholarship and pseudo-scholarship. (It would probably be more accurate to label most of its best-known works as belonging to the "It Did So Happen!" school, however.) The Garden of Eden, the remains of Noah's ark atop Mount Ararat, Moses's "Mountain of God," the actual Sea of Reeds that the Israelites crossed on their way to freedom—all of these have been somehow "located" by all sorts of well-meaning people—and by a parallel group of self-serving charlatans—as a way of "proving" the Bible to be true (and of selling a lot of books) for so long that the whole endeavor almost has the feel of a kind of cottage industry to it. The use to which Scripture can be put to sell books cannot, however, be deemed to have much to do with the way Bible study can actually bring the rationally faithful closer to God. For people in this latter category, the historicity of any particular Bible story—that is to say, the truth of the historical details presented in it—neither adds nor takes away from its spiritual worth. Indeed, for people intent on seeking God through the contemplation of Scripture, the fact that a given story itself exists is far more significant than the question of whether some specific detail within the story is or isn't historically accurate.

There is, therefore, no particular reason to consider a biblical text to be worthless merely because scientific study has yielded the conclusion that some specific detail in the story it tells does not correspond to historical reality, or that none of its details do. Unless a reader is prepared to argue that the author of a biblical story wrote specifically to mislead its readers, it is far more logical to consider biblical stories as attempts by their authors to create a set of literary compositions that would convey a specific set of beliefs and principles to readers through the medium of narrative. As a result, the question of the historicity of a specific biblical tale—and particularly one presented as part of a book of prophecy, which category includes the Torah and most of the other books in the biblical canon—will only be of decisive interest to people who feel that believing that the stories of Scripture were preserved for future generations because of their great spiritual lessons must necessarily *also* entail believing that the historical events mentioned in them are described with total accuracy.

That kind of over-focusing on the historical correctness of the text, however, will be a counterproductive exercise for most, one as little rooted in a reasonable sense of what the text *is* as it is almost guaranteed to lead readers away from a useful sense of the devotional worth of the specific chapter under consideration. This is implied in the verse from Jeremiah in which the prophet is depicted as hearing God speaking to him and telling him to "write down all the words I shall say to you in a book (Jeremiah 30:2.)" The prophet is not bidden to write down what he perceives of the world around him—and neither is he commanded to compose an essay about the geopolitics of his day or to write a poem or a sermon—but rather to write down "in ink and in a book" (36:18) whatever he is able to translate of God's communicative presence into the language of human beings . . . and nothing else. To evaluate his efforts centuries later *not* in terms of the degree to which he succeeded in doing just that—in creating a literary text that would focus his experience of God's meaningful presence through the prism of language—but rather in terms of whether the details preserved in his text "really" happened precisely as told is not to understand the nature of prophetic literature or why the text is so insistent on attributing the entire Torah to Moses, the greatest of all prophets "whom God knew face to face" (Deuteronomy 34:10) and whose entire literary oeuvre—the Torah itself—therefore demands to be taken—and analyzed—as one long prophetic oracle.

Chapter 3

THE FIRST DOMINO

Embracing paradox does not require living in a delusional world.

It is, for example, logically impossible to conceive of a situation in which two absolutely true statements contradict each other to the extent that the acceptance of one must absolutely preclude the acceptance of the other. It is also impossible to imagine a situation that requires denying truth to accept truth—all true statements, by definition, being necessarily congruent with all other true statements—and surely the burden of proof would rest, and weigh heavily, on the shoulders of any who would deny any of these assertions. As a result, the claim so often made that spiritual or religious truths are somehow different in quality and kind from scientific truths and that, therefore, it is somehow *not* impossible to conceive of a situation in which an honest individual affirms as true a dogmatic remark that that individual personally considers impossible to square with scientific reality—such a line of thinking will not be granted much credence by anyone who takes the concept of truth seriously at all. As a result, commentators who consciously interpret the biblical text according to assumptions and beliefs that they do not actually consider to be true in the ultimate, unadulterated sense of the word because of some perceived obligation to support other dogmas and doctrines (which, presumably, will be dismissed by readers as absurdities if the first domino were to be permitted to fall)—such authors, by writing things about God that even they *themselves* do not consider to be accurate or true, deprive their work of stature, importance, and worth.

BIBLE PEOPLE

A good rule of thumb to embrace is the supposition that statements about the Bible that, if they were to be made about any other book would be dismissed as self-serving fantasies, are probably not true. For example, essays rooted in the fantasy that reading a book is something like conducting a séance with the characters and personalities who appear in that book are good illustrations of this point. Yet people write and preach all the time about biblical personalities as though they were in ongoing psychic contact with them and, as a result, feel themselves to be fully capable of revealing all sorts of things about them that no one else knows or has ever known.

In any other context, this approach would be considered a kind of craziness, yet it is tolerated, even celebrated, within the world of devotional biblical literature. For honest readers, however, the bottom line will always be that it is irrational—and, indeed, impossible—to come into some sort of preternatural spiritual contact with the personalities who appear in the Bible merely by worshipfully reading their stories.

The personalities with whom it *is* conceivable to commune intellectually by reading Bible stories, however, do exist—they are the authors of the various literary texts in which we find those stories presented to us. Furthermore, because we are speaking about the authors of stories and not about the characters in those stories, the reasonableness of this approach to Scripture is unrelated to the historicity of the details in the story itself.

Any attempt, for example, to "know" Moses outside of the framework of the biblical texts in which he appears as a literary character is pointless because he exists today solely within the literary context of those stories in the first place. In other words, the extraordinary figure who lives on even today in Jewish consciousness as the greatest prophet of God who ever lived—and whom God knew "face to face" (Exodus 33:11) and to whom God spoke plainly "as one person might speak to another" (ibid.) rather than obscurely via visions or dreams (Numbers 12:6)—that figure is the literary personality called Moses in the biblical tales that relate the details of his story and not the historical individual named Moses, who is wholly unknown to us *except* through the medium of the various texts that tell his tale. Many will argue precisely to the contrary, but what proof can they offer?

THE ORIGINAL POINT

There are different categories of lies people tell about the Bible, some rooted specifically in arrogance and others more in ignorance. Strangest of all, however, would have to be arguments to the effect that the original authors of biblical texts did not actually understand their own work at its most basic level of meaning.

In the absence of proof to the contrary, honest readers will always work on the assumption that the authors of scriptural texts wished to write precisely what they did write . . . and that they wrote down precisely what they wished to convey to their readers, including both their contemporaries and whatever readers they may have realized could conceivably still be considering their work centuries, or even millennia, in the future. That authors can consciously embed obscurely coded secrets in the texts they compose is surely true, but it remains a cardinal principle of honest biblical exegesis that such an assertion must be proven categorically, not merely asserted forcefully or repeatedly.

MYTHOLOGY

Despite the incredible frustration a person of integrity attempting to explain a biblical text will inevitably feel in admitting that more or less nothing of consequence can be known today about the author of the text under consideration, reason nevertheless forbids such a reader from transferring the characteristics and traits of the personalities described in a given scriptural story to the author of that text . . . and how much the less so to its editor or to the creator of the anthology of texts in which it was preserved! You can prove this categorically with reference to yourself, incidentally. Imagine you were hired by a publisher of university-level textbooks to create an anthology of poetry by medieval Irish monks. You might well take the job—but would that make you Irish? Or medieval? Or a monk? Yet people make analogous assumptions about the authors of biblical texts all the time!

It is precisely because students of Scripture feel such an overpowering urge to engage with the biblical text that they must exercise the necessary self-control, always, to make a firm distinction between the flesh-and-blood authors of the texts under consideration and the historical or ahistorical personalities who appear in those texts as literary characters. There is nothing seamy or indecent about musing about the characters that appear in literary works, only about people who fail to accept that that is what they are doing.

MIDRASH

Midrash is the Hebrew word for "exegesis"—the literary technique by means of which a scholar is able to draw didactic, moral, or dogmatic lessons from a given section of the biblical text. These lessons may legitimately be developments of ideas actually found in the text, but they can also constitute levels of meaning that would have struck the original authors of those texts as foreign, perhaps even as incomprehensible. The value and authenticity of the midrashic process, therefore, depends fully on the integrity of the scholar proposing to use that process to make an honest point. Using midrashic technique to buttress an argument or to support a contention is, therefore, fully reasonable. Using that same set of techniques to prove that you have uncovered the "real" meaning of a text when you have no specific way of knowing if your interpretation does or doesn't correspond to the original intention of that text's author, on the other hand, is to skate on very thin ice indeed. Indeed, any interpretation of a biblical text must be judged flawed once its interpreters lose track of reality and begin to insist that they are somehow possessed of the supernatural ability to know things about ancient authors that they have no actual way of learning. When put that way, such an approach sounds ridiculous. But how many interpreters of how many countless texts have fallen precisely into that very trap?

ALONE AND TOGETHER

It is one thing to say that, taken all together in all their variety and breadth of literary style and expression, the chapters of Scripture form a kind of exalted guidebook capable of assisting people seeking to know God, but it is also reasonable to ask whether such a guidebook should exist in the first place. You could, after all, just as plausibly argue that individuals prepared to devote years, even decades, to seeking the knowledge of God should far more reasonably be encouraged to find their own paths forward and not merely to follow ones previously created by others.

There are, probably, many different answers to that question, but—to speak of what I know—the Jewish one is that any who yearn wholeheartedly to live their lives out in the shadow of God's presence will do well to think of themselves as travelers in a weird and unfamiliar wilderness no less uncharted than uncharitable . . . at the same time it is virtually indistinguishable from the world in which that same seeker lives with the rest of humanity.

Would-be pilgrims hoping to arrive one day in Jerusalem will therefore not get far by imagining themselves to be travelers on a well-paved highway without exit ramps or turn-offs that they can simply follow until eventually arriving at their final destination. Instead, seekers of God in the world will do best to think of themselves as nearsighted travelers wandering aimlessly in a world filled with roads but along which the road signs are all written in a personal language meant solely for them, but which they do not actually speak or have practical idea how to learn.

The chapters of Scripture can serve such would-be pilgrims as a kind of primer from which to learn the grammar and vocabulary of that individual-specific language, but not in the sense that all who slavishly follow the rules set down in the Bible will automatically be granted entry visas to the kingdom of God: being able to read the signs along a road is not at all the same as actually traveling that road forward to a desired destination. The Bible can indeed be such people's guidebook, but only in the sense that the traditional scriptural media of symbol, myth, statute, and commandment can make it possible for would-be pilgrims to wander their lonely, personal highways toward God in the company of countless other lonely travelers, not in the sense that embracing the Bible and punctiliously obeying its rules somehow obviates the need to journey forward at all.

STUDY

More than as a book of laws or stories, Scripture is best conceptualized as a song that can bear interpretation on a multiplicity of levels, an interpretive direction we can find suggested in the Bible itself by comparing two texts from the book of Deuteronomy.

The first is the one in which we read that, while perched at the very edge of his life, "Moses wrote out this song on that very day and taught it to the Israelites" (Deuteronomy 31:22), a verse Jewish commentators have always interpreted as a reference to Moses writing out the entire Torah before he died atop Mount Nebo. The other is a far more famous verse known to all regular synagogue worshipers that comes from the other end of that same biblical book, "And *this* is the Torah that Moses placed before the Israelites" (Deuteronomy 4:44), which can be taken as a subtle hint to the effect that there is a different Torah than the one Moses placed before all Israel, one that is wholly allusion and poetic inference and that exists just behind and beyond the parchment of the scroll Moses composed at the end of his life and bequeathed to the Jewish people as their eternal patrimony. This "other" Torah is the one that is inscribed upon the walls of the human heart that yearns for God, the one of which Jeremiah spoke when he said in the name of God, "I shall grant them My *torah* / I shall write it on their hearts" (Jeremiah 31:32). It is the Torah outside of the strictures of language, the one that functions in the world as the redemptive energy that surges through individuals seeking to know God through the informed, intense study of texts that *themselves* are the product of earlier individuals' attempts to funnel their experience of the living God through the triple prism of consciousness, perception, and language. Studying Scripture means stepping into *that* bracing stream and is, therefore, an undertaking for neither the fainthearted nor the lazy—and certainly not for people afraid of getting their feet wet.

Chapter Four

The Fourth Gate

Praying to God

In the minds of most people, there is no activity more emblematic of the enterprise of religion than prayer. That it doesn't really work—at least not in the way everyone wishes it would—seems almost blasphemous for anyone, let alone a rabbi, to say out loud. That it rests on the theological supposition that God is capable and willing to listen to the prayers of countless millions of faithful worshipers day in and day out for millennia without losing interest (and presumably also without suffering a concomitant diminution of divine compassion) does not appear to make it less appealing to people who take such divine interest in their own personal lives for granted. Finally, although the notion that participating in prayer enables the faithful to approach God as though the Almighty were a celestial candy machine capable of dispensing all the best treats when the right combination of coins is pushed into its slot rings more silly than sinful, that is precisely how prayer was and still is explained to most people in the context of their religious education or training. And the fact that no one—or surely almost no one—*actually* expects the desired candy bar to pop out only makes the appeal of prayer even more mysterious.

In short, nothing *feels* less reasonable than mumbling your deepest hopes and wishes into your shirt and then professing amazement when the Master of Being doesn't hop to it and grant those wishes and realize those hopes. And yet, paradoxically, the more seriously people take the whole enterprise, the less troublesome the fact that prayer doesn't produce—or hardly *ever* produces—the desired effect seems to become. When you order eggs in a restaurant and the waiter either forgets entirely about the order or else becomes confused and brings oatmeal instead, it's entirely normal to be irritated. But when someone prays for remission and gets metastasis, the expectation is that the patient's response should feature above all calm stoicism born of faith, that it would constitute some sort of moral failure to stop believing in the sublime efficacy of prayer merely because a sick person prayed to God for healing and yet remained ill. In such cases, clergypeople of all stripes smugly offer up pap like "the fact that the answer was no doesn't mean that the prayer wasn't answered" and they get away with it too. But if prayer were medicine, most of us would have found new doctors a long time ago.

And yet . . . the world is full of people who have found the path to God to lead through the experience of prayer. The landscape of prayer—its words and tunes, its nuances and spoken (and unspoken) implications, its whispered hopes and voiced (and unvoiced) aspirations—this wholly evocative landscape serves as the backdrop against which millions seek communion with the living God every day of their lives and find great satisfaction in doing so. It surely doesn't work simply or well—and even people who have adopted a daily regimen of prayer would surely agree, or most of them would, that parents who insist on treating their children's leukemia with prayer instead medical intervention are not just negligent, but criminally so—but the notion of speaking to God through the medium of prayer is still what makes God's presence real for countless people on this earth. They aren't all deranged, surely. But what precisely then *is* this gate through which so many pass on their way to faith? And how can you pass through it without surrendering your intellectual pride and spiritual integrity? Those are the questions to ask as we approach this great gateway looming before us and inviting us, if we dare, to pass through it without sacrificing what we know on the altar of what we wish.

THE POINT OF PRAYER

For Jews, the problem is marginally less acute because Judaism teaches that a prayer is not just plea or petition, but a *mitzvah*—a commandment like all the others that exists primarily to move an individual forward toward the great goal of living a life in God. And, indeed, those who address God in prayer without ruining their efforts with self-interest, conceit, or arrogance may actually find themselves trembling when seized by the candor that exists at the confluence of humility and honesty in the context of prayer. That trembling is crucial too: for most, it is the first sign that someone has embraced prayer as an exercise in spiritual growth rather than as an opportunity to whine. It is most definitely something to work toward and to feel accomplished upon achieving. And it is certainly attainable, to which possibility attest the psalmist's words "Fear and trembling have seized me" (Psalm

55:6). But it is not at all easy to feel God's presence so intensely that it produces an actual physical effect, and that really is to say the very least.

On the other hand, those who come before God in prayer in the manner of people entering a shop and reading out to the shopkeeper the list of things they have come to purchase . . . and who then complain that their prayers were not answered or, even more pathetically, who become outraged that they were not appropriately rewarded for the great devotion with which they recited their prayers or for their deep knowledge of liturgy and hymnody—to such people, the Torah unsentimentally says that "God will hear the sound of your words and become enraged" (Deuteronomy 1:34). This does not mean that there is something perverse or base about approaching God in petitionary prayer or supplication. But it does mean that the point of doing so must never be personal gain but rather the opportunity to know God more intimately, more deeply and more intensely, through the medium of speech directed toward the listening ear of a caring, personal God.

Prayer is only one of many commandments recorded in the Torah, but its point is precisely the same as the point of all the other commandments: to help an individual create a context in which to cleave unto God. It therefore follows that those whose prayers are not the expression *solely* of spiritual longing cannot consider themselves to have performed the commandment to lift up their hearts in prayer to God at all and, indeed, have debased the concept of prayer by using it as an avenue toward self-gratification and personal gain. It is a truth no less awful than foundational that God cannot be bought or bribed with prayer, but this does not imply that the human soul cannot be mightily elevated through the experience of prayer. That certainly *is* true—as witness the untold numbers of people who have indeed come to know God through the medium of prayer.

IDIOSYNCRASIS

Does anybody really imagine that the commandment to lift up our hearts to God in prayer can be fulfilled by muttering a few words someone else once wrote? Does anyone not find it comical to imagine someone attempting to express deep yearning for God in the manner of a simpleton attempting to awaken passionate love in the heart of another by reading aloud borrowed love notes someone else once wrote to the object of that person's passionate desire? Can prayer that does not come from the specific heart of the specific individual at prayer even be considered prayer in any but the most formal sense of the word?

These are all rhetorical questions, their answers wholly obvious. People, therefore, who wish to build a bridge between themselves and God using the tools of language and literary expression must first learn how to introduce enough of their creative energy into every syllable of prayer they utter to transform those prayers into fully personal, totally idiosyncratic utterances that have never before been spoken and which never again will be spoken by anyone else . . . including not by the speakers themselves. Can moderns do it? Even the least creative among us somehow find it possible to invest ourselves fully in the words we use to invite a lover to bed . . . and somehow to call those words up from within our own creative consciousnesses without having to read a script someone else once wrote as an expression of personal yearning for a different partner. Indeed, why exactly it is that people who can find it in them to speak from the heart to a lover find it so difficult to utter even a single syllable of prayer fully invested with passion, yearning, and the full focus of their desire to encounter God is the exact question that lies at the heart of the matter.

On the other hand, it seems rational to argue that the commandment of Scripture to love God with a full heart is based on the assumption that God created physical, sensual love in the first place so as to give to humanity an easily accessible model of the kind of passion and desire which people should feel called to bring to their various acts of religious observance, most definitely including prayer. In turn, this is the most basic meaning of the poet's injunction, "Worship God with *simḥah*" (Psalm 100:2), in which verse the Hebrew word *simḥah* is a subtle reference to the love of lovers, as is clear from the passage in Deuteronomy that tells the newlywed man in a time of war *not* to join the army immediately, but rather to remain home "and provide *simḥah* to the wife he has taken" (Deuteronomy 24:5).

THE MOST INTIMATE COMMANDMENT

In order to bring forth one single syllable of honest prayer from their mouths, individuals at prayer must accept—and recall constantly—that the only kind of prayer than can come before the exalted heavenly throne on which God sits to receive the prayers of the pious is the wordless prayer that exists solely as the extra-linguistic embodiment of wholehearted yearning for God . . . and this is the truth to which the prophet alluded when, using a hybrid divine name that appears dozens of times in Scripture, he exhorted his listeners to "be silent before Adonai-Elohim" (Zephaniah 1:7). And it is also the great truth that the poet whose ode to faith we call the sixty-second psalm meant to convey by opening his poem with the remarkable assertion that the path to redemption may well not be best pursued through speech at all, even of the most exalted variety, but rather through silence.

Honest prayer flows out of the mouth of the individual at prayer into the world, but originates in longing for God that is as pure as it is free from any hint of self-interest . . . and which, in turn, has *its* origin in several places: in an interior fund of deep humility and modesty that the praying individual brings to the enterprise, in the sense of inexplicable wonder the honest supplicant will inevitably feel welling up deep within when risking to speak a word in confidence to God, and in the deep-seated conviction all truly honest worshipers feel that they are risking everything by daring to consider themselves sufficiently meritorious to stand in prayer before God in the first place.

On the other hand, even the most expertly executed prayer will inevitably be ruined by presumptuousness and smugness. And, indeed, the ability to pray humbly and wholly without pretense will come naturally to almost none at all. That is surely a shame, but it hardly negates the prophet's reassuring message regarding people who do somehow manage to make themselves capable of approaching God in prayer untainted by self-interest, a message featuring God's promise that "they shall call on My name and I shall hear them" (Zachariah 13:9).

When people tell me they send their children to synagogue because they want them to learn how to pray, I can only smile. I've been saying my prayers three times daily for my entire adult life and I'd like to learn how to do it too.

THE TASTE OF CELERY

Part of the problem with prayer is that it is inevitably couched in human language. But the languages of the world are so wanting in terms of descriptive ability that even the simplest things are commonly considered more or less wholly inexpressible in words. And, indeed, it really would be impossible to use mere words to explain to a blind person what a red hat looks like or to explain to someone with no olfactory sensitivity what the precise difference is between the way apple and peach blossoms smell, let alone to tell someone what it feels like to break your ankle. Or how old age feels. Or what it feels like to fall in love.

It is in the context of this shallowness of language that we must approach the concept of prayer as well: the individual at prayer is generally looking to words that fail utterly when it comes to describing the taste of celery or the feel of slightly frozen snow under foot and expecting them adequately to express the longing the worshiper feels for God in all its depth and pathos. Yet, for all it is patently absurd to imagine anyone *ever* succeeding at such a wildly improbable undertaking, it is also the case that prayer derives its profundity precisely from the fact that it is only *almost* impossible, not entirely or absolutely so. And so we come to two truly off-putting truths that all who would approach God in prayer must face. One is that it will take years, perhaps even decades, to develop the sense of humility requisite for even marginal success. And the other is that there are definitely those who will come closest to meaningful prayer by saying nothing at all in accordance with the psalmist's observation that "to You, God in Zion, silence alone is [true] praise" (Psalm 65:2).

PRAYER AS EXERCISE

People who pray to God at the same time they are convinced that God will not answer them or respond to their prayers—or that God for some reason actually cannot respond to the prayers of human beings in a clear, unequivocal way—such people are the people to whom the prophet was making reference when he spoke of "the deranged of spirit" (Hosea 9:7) because they are engaging in an effort even they themselves do not believe will bear any fruit.

People who pray to God at the same time they are convinced that there exists the possibility that God will answer them, but that that possibility is so remote that it would be ridiculous to expect it to come about in any substantive way at all—such people are either fools or hopeless romantics . . . and "prolonged hope is a disease of the heart" (Proverbs 13:12).

And, finally, people who pray to God at the same time they are convinced absolutely and unequivocally that God will answer their prayers in just the way for which they are hoping—such people are living in a dream world and, for all they may admire themselves for the steadfast trust they bring to the enterprise, are in fact guilty of trivializing the larger concept of prayer by ignoring the way it actually functions in the world of real people, and thus also of not really taking it very seriously at all.

The deepest meaning of prayer lies in the fact that, at its most refined and significant, prayer can be understood as a kind of intense spiritual exercise, one that may be used slowly to inculcate the lesson that God exists in a potential relationship with every single human being neither *solely* as a monarch who rules over the world nor *solely* as a judge poised to pronounce sentence, but also as a willing partner in dialogue and as a caring, devoted friend.

THE NAMES OF GOD

I've written above about the inadequacy of language, but it also bears saying that there is also something profoundly powerful, albeit negatively so, in the use of language at all as the context in which to address God. This, Scripture teaches subtly by inviting readers to puzzle over the relationship between two verses in Scripture: the one in which God tells to Adam to "rule over the fishes of the sea and the birds of the sky and over all the beasts that crawl along the dry land" (Genesis 1:28) and the other in which it is reported that

Adam did so precisely by "assigning names to all animal life, to the birds of the sky and all beasts of the field" (Genesis 2:20). Prayer situations that feature human beings speaking to God in their own language, or in any language, or that call upon people to use words to praise God are therefore at best dicey undertakings. References to the greatness of God abound in Scripture and have the ring of compliment and praise, of course. But what greater act of human hubris could there be than attempting to capture anything at all of God within the confines of human language? Indeed, by insisting that speaking the praises of God is our obligation and surely thus also our right, are we not inadvertently, if futilely, doing to God what Adam did to the beasts of the field and the birds of the sky? And yet the daily obligation to lift up our hearts in prayer is not only permitted, but actually ordained by Scripture. (Jewish readers will want to know as well that that specific obligation—to lift up our hearts in prayer daily to God—is indeed counted as one of the 613 commandments.) Could it then be that Scripture makes the concept of daily prayer into a divine commandment precisely because the effort to use human language to engage with God, and all the more so to praise God, would otherwise border on blasphemy? That surely could be the case! And the lesson to learn from that is that the only acceptable way to approach God in prayer is humbly, and imbued with the sense that the right to pray is a divinely granted privilege. Daily prayer is therefore not a gift of humankind to God, but precisely *vice versa*.

LANGUAGE AND PRAYER

God is described in the Bible as heaping ridicule and scorn on the simple-minded types in ancient times who imagined that the Almighty somehow actually ate the meat of the various sacrifices offered up on the great bronze altar in the Temple in Jerusalem or drank the endless gallons of blood poured out on that altar as libation offerings . . . and this is the simple meaning of the pointed questions the Psalmist cites in the name of God: "Do I *really* eat the flesh of oxen? Do I *really* drink the blood of rams?" (Psalm 50:13). But no less naïve are people in our own day who use words derived from the human experience (which includes all words in all languages) piously to say anything at all about God.

To the extent that human language by its very nature is rooted in human experience and in the specific, limited way we human beings perceive our world and decipher it through our various senses, it is reasonable to say that everything that any human being says about God is made meaningless the moment it is encapsulated in words of any sort, and this is true regardless of how fervently that individual holds that specific belief to be true. This is a core idea, one in the contemplation of which rests the key to adopting a theology of prayer that bears meaning outside the boundless conceit of the individual at prayer. Moreover, only those who clear that hurdle may pass through the gate of prayer and, in so doing, come that much closer to God through the medium of the spoken word.

Chapter Five

The Fifth Gate

Worshiping God

Just as the search for "love" absent any real interest in actually loving a specific person is doomed to be pointless and dissatisfying, so is it equally meaningless for us to yearn for faith without focusing our longing on some concept, however simple, of what God is. It is an easy trap to fall into, however, because both the pleasure and the pageantry of ritual, especially when experienced together, are more than capable of obscuring the slightly daunting—and more than slightly dour—truth that worship undertaken for its own sake will never be anything more than an exercise in self-gratification. That isn't to say that there is necessarily something base or ignoble in the enjoyment of worship. Just to the contrary, actually: nothing could be more natural than for those drawn to the worship of God to enjoy the experience, just as it is natural for people to enjoy undertaking the various acts of kindness and caring they perform to make the people in their lives whom they truly love aware of the depth of the feelings they have for them. Passing through the gate of worship on the great journey to God surely does not mean, then, perversely disciplining ourselves *not* to enjoy the rituals and rites of formal worship, but rather willing ourselves productively and meaningfully to use those rituals as an way of opening our hearts to God, of making ourselves vulnerable in the manner of lovers who find in baring their souls to each other the ultimate path toward intimacy. (In religion, as in romantic love, true intimacy is almost invariably born of the heady admixture of self-assuredness and vulnerability. That's why teenagers are so much better at sex than love—because sex requires opportunity, but love requires confidence.)

Worshiping God with integrity means rooting your decision to follow all sorts of picayune rules and regulations *not* because you fear being punished for having failed to perform the ritual in question absolutely properly, but as a function of your natural willingness to stand shoulder-to-shoulder with all engaged similarly in the great effort of translating the love of God from theory into practice, from the brain to the arm, from the world of ideas into the physical world of real things. Although an inordinate amount of time is spent in more or less *every* faith community trying to convince children that worship is fun, the awful truth is that worship is work, and difficult work at that. (It is not mere coincidence that the Hebrew word *avodah* is used to denote both daily labor and divine service.) Worship thus requires the coordination of the inner and outer selves, of spirit and flesh, of the heart *and* the mind *and* the arm *and* the leg. It is directed toward God—in Hebrew, as in all Western languages, the verb "to worship" takes a divine direct object almost naturally—but worship is far less *about* God than it is *about* the worshiper, far less a manifestation of divine will than the willful expression of those who undertake to express themselves in deed no less eloquently than in word. It takes a lifetime to do it right—and no one ever *really* does it fully and absolutely right, to which truth the uncountable number of books devoted to fleshing out the minutiae of Jewish law mutely attest—but even the simplest, least elegant act of worship has the capacity to alter the way God is understood and perceived, and thus also the way God exists in the personal ambit of the worshiper. And in that way too is worship like love.

HONEST WORSHIP

At its simplest, worship is the act of walking toward God along a path paved with words and deeds. For a Jew, these words are the words of the Torah of Moses, also known in biblical texts as the Torah of God, and the deeds are the rituals presented there as the commandments of a God who cares best of all to be approached within the context of symbolic gesture. (Why that may be, Scripture declines to explain. Maybe it's just practical that a God who can only be described metaphorically be approached only symbolically.) But whatever the ultimate logic behind the system may be, the rituals of worship may themselves be expressed symbolically as rungs on a ladder akin to the ladder reaching from earth to heaven that Jacob saw in his night vision at Beth El. The image is famous, but by depicting Jacob as Everyman—and by painting him as a complicated, imperfect soul—Scripture seems to be saying that such a ladder can exist for any who wish to ascend toward the knowledge of God by embracing the rituals and rites ordained by Scripture. Jacob is depicting as responding to his own vision by pledging to build a temple to God on that spot and that detail too fits into the larger picture easily: by depicting Jacob's response in that specific way, Scripture is suggesting that it is possible for real people in the real world—and not just in the ethereal context of spiritual theory—to encounter the divine through the medium of worship in personal temples built with their own hands in their own places, and as expressions of their personal will to worship God in that place.

To the extent that honest worship has the capacity to lead the worshiper to a palpable sense of intimacy with God, divine service can surely be a force for great good in the spiritual life of the individual. However, the influence of worship on the worshiper can also be malign and, indeed, venerating the commandments of the Torah as anything other than ritualized expressions of the desire an individual possesses to come one step closer to communion with God through the medium of worship and ritual will always be counterproductive. As a result, engaging in worship as a means of forcing—or, rather, of attempting to force—God to provide this or that boon to the performer of the commandment (or to his or her family or to anyone at all) will in almost every case come to naught. And it is precisely that kind of greedy worship that Scripture condemns in the strongest terms as spiritual lechery, which lesson comes through all too clearly in the trenchant remark of the prophet Hosea to the effect that those in his day who knew not God, knew God not *not* because they declined to participate in formal worship, but "because a whorish spirit was in them" (Hosea 5:4) and that spirit ruined their worship by making it about their own personal gratification.

The only truly essential difference between the kind of worship Hosea condemned and the true worship of God rests in the degree to which the worshipers do or do not all allow themselves to be motivated primarily by egotism and the urge to self-aggrandize. Students of the Mishnah will recognize this thought in the ancient words of Antigonos of Sokho, who taught his followers to be "not as slaves who serve their master in order to receive a reward, but rather as slaves who serve their master without any interest in whatever reward they may subsequently receive" (M. Avot 1:3). In Antigonos's estimation, then, the legitimate worshiper is the one who serves God out of a sense of awe and reverence rather than out of any hope of receiving even the least significant of God's blessings in return and this will surely be the case for moderns as well.

The commandments of the Torah may *also* be thought of as wordless prayers and their performance as the wordless praise of God that inspired the psalmist to write the verse that serves me personal as a kind of mantra: "To You, God in Zion, is silence *alone* praise" (Psalm 65:2). Indeed, just as no words can fully describe the praise due to God, so can no commandment—each one a soundless word spoken outside the context of language—adequately express the yearning of its performer to know God through ritual. Declining to pray because mere words are unable fully to express the awe any of us might feel with respect to the majesty of the divine would seem a peculiar response to the inadequacy of language, however. And the same is surely true regarding wordless prayer as well.

Chapter 5
WORSHIP AND HOLINESS

The commandments exist as words in a book and then, if they are translated from the realm of language to the realm of deeds, as physical acts in the world of people and things. This is the sum total of their reality, however: other than as theoretical or realized ritual acts (depending on whether they are being contemplated or undertaken), they have no existential stature of any sort at all and will only be imagined to exist other than as words in a book or actions undertaken in the world by people unclear on the concept of worship. Furthermore, all too are in error who claim that the sacred nature of the commandments derives from some source of theoretical holiness embedded deep within their detail rather than from the fact that they have the potential to serve as a narrow but real bridge between those who perform them and the God Scripture repeatedly references as the Holy One of Israel. To someone possessed of true spiritual integrity, the performance of a commandment can never be an end unto itself.

To say the same thing in different words, the commandments of the Torah are sacred because they possess the uncanny ability to be translated by those who perform them from words in a book into deeds that can lead to God . . . *if* they are successfully invested with sufficient internal passion to make them into footsteps of motionless movement on a journey without physical trajectory or destination toward communion with a divine realm that exists outside of time and space. In that sense, the commandments may well feel like magical doorways through which worshipers are self-enabling themselves to step. Absent a deep sense of personal readiness to understand the specific act under consideration solely as an act intended to make finer or better an individual's effort to worship God, however, the commandments of Scripture will serve as little more than vehicles for that individual's self-promotion. And yet it is also so that worship—when undertaken in the context of abject humility and spiritual yearning untainted by egotism and the desire to self-aggrandize—can indeed lead to God, which truth is evidenced ably by the countless generations of souls who have found God through faithful and detailed obedience to the commandments of Scripture.

The rewards of worship undertaken in humility and total candor are great. And, indeed, any who succeed at transforming the commandments of the Torah from the realm of mere possibility to the domain of real deeds possessed of inarguable spiritual worth are called true worshipers of God and become able to move closer to God through the fulfillment of the commandments of Scripture in the way they were intended all along to function in the world. By doing so, then, such people also fulfill the poet's injunction to "take [their] offering and go to the courtyards of God's temple" (Psalm 96:8)—that is to say: to take their offering—which term here refers to the pure, selfless desire to serve God that lives deep within the inmost chambers of every human heart—and to use that offering to animate their ritual deeds, thereby making them as worthy and acceptable before God as the sacrifices the ancients brought to the courtyards of the Jerusalem Temple. The Bible speaks of the free-will offering of an unblemished animal as symbolic of personal willingness to subordinate the tasks of daily life to the search *for* God and to the worship *of* God. But the image of lonely pilgrims ending their journey to God by entering the Temple courtyards to offer up sacrificial animals on the altar is only one of the many ways Scripture refers to the worship of God that may take place in any time and in any setting.

THE MOST IMPORTANT COMMANDMENT

Every student of Scripture will eventually wonder what the single most important commandment is and, indeed, the Talmud presents any number of stories about rabbis who felt called to debate which commandment, or which several few commandments, is or are the most essential and basic one or ones. (Interested readers will find them conveniently concentrated in the Talmudic tractate called Makkot on pages 23b and 24a.) I suppose, in the end, there will be as many different answers to that question as there are people trying to answer it, but, at least for me, the most essential commandment in the Torah of Moses is "Be guileless before God" (Deuteronomy 18:13). Speaking personally, it doesn't get much more basic than that.

To begin to approach God totally without guile requires internalizing the seriously destabilizing truth that not even one single word of absolute truth about God has neither ever been written nor will or could ever be written—and especially not in any human language, each of which is a totally artificial code devised to allow the members of some national or ethnic group to communicate with each other. For that reason, speaking in broad assertions and reassuring certainties about God can be justified, at best, as a noble effort to say something that conceivably could be true. But to speak about God using the language of self-evident certainty and unshakeable assumption is close enough to lying to be forbidden under the general injunctions to "distance yourself from falsehood" (Exodus 23:7) and to refrain from talebearing, as Scripture says pointedly, "Thou shalt not go about bearing tales" (Leviticus 19:16). And the argument that making statements about God that you don't know to be true is not the same as saying things about God that you know to be untrue is a slender reed indeed upon which to hang a lifetime of pious posturing.

The meaning of the verse cited above from Deuteronomy about guilelessness is that no effort any human being makes to know God, or even to know *of* God, that is undertaken in the absence of absolute spiritual integrity and candor will lead to the God whose very name is Truth. To deny that principle is consciously to choose naiveté over insight. On the other hand, to understand that it is true but to make a virtue out of ignoring its implications is merely to trade in naiveté for cynicism, neither a gift any thinking person would wish to bring to the altar.

A SMIDGEN OF HOPE

Precisely because it sounds so logical to imagine that the commandments exist in the first place to provide the faithful with a window into the true nature of divinity, it is always essential to remember that the unfathomability of God will always be the cornerstone of all honest religion. There is a certain disconcerting feel to this principle, to be sure. In the end, however, those who insist they can do this or that thing and then magically come to know God in the simple, easy way they know their friends or neighbors are acting like demented warriors trying to break into a walled city by throwing snowflakes at its walls, then professing amazement at their failure to enter the city because, after all, they really were throwing the flakes as forcefully as they could.

The ability to travel the high road to communion with God derives, therefore, directly from the ability of a specific individual somehow to find the courage to pursue God in the almost total absence of reasonable hope that it could be possible, for *even* the briefest of moments, for a mortal being to know anything at all of God with absolute certainty.

*

Once upon a time, a prince set off on a journey to a distant land after hearing of the great beauty and goodness of a princess who lived there. The princess, however, lived in a palace that was remote and highly inaccessible. Situated in the middle of a forest filled with ferocious beasts and surrounded a huge desert, the palace itself was protected by one hundred concentric walls, each designed specifically to keep all intruders from ever penetrating its inmost precincts. Different kinds of caravans did occasionally arrive at the palace gate by various circuitous routes, but the princess, having taken an oath to accept as a suitor only someone who was able to cross both the desert and the forest and to scale all one hundred walls around her palace while barefoot, unarmed, and totally and absolutely alone, showed no interest in any of her occasional visitors. To do this thing—to cross the desert and the forest, to elude the wild beasts, to scale the walls, to arrive at the gate of the palace divested of all protection and, indeed, possessing nothing at all other than the fierce will to succeed at conquering the princess's heart—was almost impossible. But it was only almost impossible . . . and the knowledge that it was not totally and absolutely impossible gave the prince sufficient courage, and sufficient stubbornness, to continue the journey to his beloved . . . despite the fact that he had never actually met her and, in fact, only knew of her through the stories of travelers whose accounts he could only hope were reliable.

*

The almost total absence of reasonable expectation regarding the doability of the enterprise does not make it totally impossible for an individual honestly to hope for success at achieving communion *with* God and for redemption *in* God, but such hopes must be set within a vision of reality rooted in the absolute—and absolutely unwavering—integrity both of the intellect and the spirit. This is the meaning at the heart of the verse taken from Ezekiel's vision of the valley of dried bones, "Behold, they are saying, 'Our bones are dried out and our hope is gone'" (Ezekiel 37:11). One could reasonably ask why, if they had lost all hope, the people whose skeletons those desiccated bones once constituted were bothering to call out to the prophet at all! There could be many answers to that question, but I like to imagine that they cried out precisely because they had not lost hope *entirely* and so, by finding an infinitesimal smidgen of confidence buried beneath a mountain of uncertainty, became able to give voice to their yearning for redemption in an atmosphere of total candor and absolute honesty.

IDOLS

The pagan gods that were worshiped in biblical times—Baal Zebub, Baal Peor, Kemosh, Molekh, Astarte, Marduk, Zeus, Osiris, Jupiter and all the others mentioned or ignored in Scripture—have lost their ability to engage the hearts of people today and therefore have no worshipers left among the living. Nor are temples any longer built to their glory, thus bringing to fulfillment Isaiah's prediction that "the idols shall totally vanish" (Isaiah 2:18)—which is to say that the idols that the prophet observed being worshiped in his own day were destined to pass out of public view and for no one in the future to attempt to achieve communion with God by means of their worship.

Idolatry, however, does indeed exist in our own day wherever the rituals of religious worship are performed as goals unto themselves and when their observance becomes a kind of competition *with* others rather than a process leading *to* God. But, most of all, it exists when their observance blinds those performing them from the true and sole goal of legitimate divine worship, which is the veneration of the Almighty. The prophets of ancient times knew well this truth: it is what Amos meant to proclaim with the words, "Thus saith God to the House of Israel: Seek me and live" (Amos 5:4), which is to say: seek me through worship and prayer, but solely so that we might meet, even if just for the briefest moment, on the same plane of existence and not for your own ends or purposes.

Every commandment performed without the performer having as his or her sole intent the worship of God through the agency of that particular ritual act becomes the latter-day equivalent of one of the idols so loathed by the scriptural authors and, especially, by the prophets. But it wasn't only the prophets of biblical antiquity who were so negatively exercised by the phenomenon of idolatry: the psalmists hated that kind of false pietism as well. Indeed, it is regarding the perpetrators of such instances of debased worship that the same words, "May those who make them become just like them . . . and those who trust in them as well" (Psalms 115:8 and 135:18), appear in two different psalms to condemn idol and idolater. Angry words from angry poets (unless, of course, both psalms were written by the same poet), but in any event a curse rooted in a lesson no less worthwhile learning today than it was millennia ago when the psalmists lived in Jerusalem and sang their songs in the sacred precincts of the Holy Temple.

REWARDS

Despite the fact that so many people profess to find it self-evident, it's hard to think of a less likely theory than the one that posits that that God will invariably bless the pious and the righteous with the choicest of divine blessings, a point of view more or less totally negated by even a casual analysis of the way life actually works on earth. Interestingly enough, the parallel notion—that the wicked, at least eventually, receive the punishment they deserve—is also widely asserted by people eager to demonstrate the depth of their piety . . . and also totally unsubstantiated by the reality most people know.

It isn't at all hard to understand why these theories are so popular, but that does not make it any less essential for people possessed of spiritual integrity to own up to the disquieting fact that the system of reward and punishment, if it exists at all, clearly does not exist in the satisfying, *quid pro quo* manner that all fair-minded people wish it did. Insisting that such a system *must* exist because it would be convenient if it did—and, even more peculiarly, insisting that the existence of such a system should be self-evident to anyone possessed of true faith in God—must be considered evidence of an individual's willingness to pay with his or her spiritual integrity for the right to live inside a dream world of his or her own making. The Creator may indeed be perceived through the traces of the divine that inhere in creation, but only when the individuals doing the perceiving are willing to look out at the world with their eyes totally open.

The reward for the performance of a commandment is the tiny step forward toward God made through the agency of that particular commandment. In ancient times, this is the idea at the core of Ben Azzai's teaching to the effect that "the reward for the performance of a commandment is the inner strength to perform another commandment, while the wages of sin is the ease with which it then becomes possible to sin again" (M. Avot 4:2). The notion, therefore, that there is also some other reward an individual can expect to receive from God for the performance of any of the commandments is neither self-evident nor even all that likely. There is no greater challenge that faces the faithful than for them to divest themselves totally of the sense that it is noble and good to insist on the truth of things they can neither substantiate nor effectively demonstrate . . . and instead to walk humbly with God by accepting the intellectual limitations that define the human condition and then moving forward from there.

SPIRIT AND INTELLECT

Transforming a single ritual act from a hopeful gesture into an act of purposeful worship requires infusing it with enough untainted spiritual yearning for the gesture in question meaningfully to function as a guileless step forward toward communion with God. The inner strength necessary to do such a thing, however, is lacking in the vast majority of people. Indeed, the ability to perform one single commandment without any trace of haughtiness, arrogance, egotism or self-interest only comes to most after many years of spiritual exercise, if at all, yet the effort to arrive at that level of worshipful ability is key in that, in the end and after the hurly-burly's done, "the sacrifice God desires is the humbled spirit" (Psalm 51:19).

It was for this reason that Jewish law declines to impose the obligation to perform the commandments on children. This is not because it would be impossible to teach the average child how to perform a specific commandment properly, but rather because children lack the emotional maturity to move a ritual act from the realm of hopeful gesture into the realm of true worship.

For example, the law permits a child to read aloud from the Torah but not to lead the congregation in public prayer. As any regular at synagogue will know, however, reading aloud from the Torah scroll as it is chanted in the context of public worship is the more difficult skill to master, and by far. The relevant point here, however, is unrelated to the ease or difficulty of doing some specific thing, but rather to the fact that reading from the scroll is a service to the community but not an act of worship, whereas daily prayer is one of the cardinal commandments of Scripture. The issue has to do with the nature of worship itself and with the difficulty of taking an empty gesture and suffusing it totally with yearning for God, something no child, even the very brightest, could reasonably be expected to do that absent the spiritual maturity that comes, although surely not inevitably, with growth to adulthood. Perhaps this is why Jews celebrate the coming of age of their children at an age related to the onset of puberty—not because twelve- or thirteen-year-olds really *are* adults or because younger children cannot memorize rules, but because it is at that age that the ability to transform ritual into worship manifests itself in most children for the very first time. And absent that, ritual behavior is mere mimicry.

THE LOGIC OF WORSHIP

Of all the justifications moderns use to excuse laxness in observance or worship, the most familiar to any rabbi will be the one developed along the lines of an individual's claim not to "get" the point of any specific commandment. (I imagine the same must be true in other religious settings as well, but here again I write of what I know.) The assumption that lies just beneath such an assertion, however—that the worth of a worshipful act rests in its ability to be explained logically—may itself be tested in terms of its logic and will almost always be found wanting. Indeed, attempting to argue that one of the commandments lacks sufficient logic behind its detail to make it worth undertaking is not unlike challenging a musician to justify the beauty of his or her music with reference to the logic of the harmonic substructure employed by the composer of a given piece. (Such an explanation could certainly be forthcoming, but surely the beauty of the music exists independently of that kind of learned, scientific analysis, as does also its ability to inspire those listening to it or to move them.) The same could be said about works of art or acts of love, but it is no less true about the commandments of Scripture: they may surely be analyzed in terms of their mythic substructure, legal framework, or aesthetic detail, but will never successfully or meaningfully be evaluated solely in those terms.

In the end, it is no more or less logical to worship God through the sacrifice of barnyard animals or the decapitation of doves than through the lighting of Sabbath candles or through public prayer. Nor is it any more or less logical to seek God in a pile of grain left lying on the ground in the corner of a field for the poor to come and take than in the informed contemplation of the gemstones that adorned the High Priest's famous breastplate. Like love, religion defies logic, yet exists in a world that otherwise mostly conforms to the rules of logic . . . and this is neither bad nor good, but simply how things are in the world of adults who yearn for God.

Attempting to justify specific elements of any particular ritual by struggling to demonstrate the rational nature of some or all of its details will almost always be a counterproductive undertaking. Indeed, the only rationale necessary to justify a specific worshipful act undertaken with a full heart is the demonstration that the act in question has the ability to function as a kind of lens through which may be focused, and ideally also magnified, a previously less clearly focused and less intense sense of spiritual longing for God on the part of the individual performing the act under consideration. No more than that, but also no less!

SELFLESSNESS

Even the most casual student of Scripture will immediately see that the commandments differ in terms of the ease with which they may be performed. Some require strenuous effort, whereas others demand hardly any physical effort at all. Some require huge outlays of cash to do properly, but others require the expenditure of little or no money at all. Some take up vast amounts of time properly to undertake (or even to undertake at all), while others can be accomplished successfully in just a few moments. In the end, though, evaluating the commandments other than in an *ex post facto* way with respect to the degree to which they were or were not successful in assisting the people undertaking them to grow spiritually through their agency makes no more sense than evaluating a sonnet in terms of the number of times some specific letter of the alphabet appears in it. That detail is surely a real fact (or at least a real factoid), but it is nonetheless totally irrelevant to the question at hand because the only meaningful way to evaluate a poem is to consider its ability to affect its readers' understanding of whatever notion or emotion the poet was attempting to stimulate in them by composing the poem in the first place.

It is essential to understand—and to accept wholeheartedly—that it is rare, not common (and certainly not automatic), to succeed at the performance of any given commandment. As a result, any who do succeed at worship are called righteous and their acts of worship are called guileless and pure . . . but even people whose entire lives are given over to the cultivation of ritual will find it almost impossible solely to engage in worship that is totally selfless. Worship is burdensome. It can also be off-putting, time-consuming, and anxiety-producing. In the end, though, only guileless worship divested of ulterior motive and unrelated to the self-image of the worshiper makes it possible for religion to exist as a force for good in the real world of actual people.

The bottom line is that it takes decades, not minutes, of meditative effort to perform even the simplest of commandments in a totally selfless way as part of a regimen of mindful spiritual observance that is itself sufficiently pure and devoid of self-interest reasonably to be called guileless. As a result, many who commit to ritual observance never succeed even despite the level of enthusiasm they bring to the undertaking. On the other hand, it is precisely because success is not guaranteed that there is such nobility in even attempting to know God through the medium of worship.

CONTENT, NOT FORM

Diligence and exactitude in the observance of the commandments do not constitute any sort of protection against spiritual self-deception. Indeed, those who worship God through the punctilious observance *of* the commandments, but who, at the same time, hide from God behind a fence fashioned of lies and half-truths *about* the commandments cannot reasonably be said to be accomplishing anything particularly meritorious at all.

Worship that is devoid of meaningful inner content is called in the Bible by the general term of "iniquity" and its proponents are called "doers of iniquity" and their temples, "sites of iniquity." This is what the prophet Amos meant when he wrote that Bethel would become a site of iniquity (Amos 5:5): not that Bethel was to be destroyed or that God would no longer be worshiped in the royal sanctuary in that place, but that God would be worshiped there by dissemblers whose faith was all of it in their mouths and none of it in their hearts, and whose worship was totally formalized and devoid of inner content or meaning. The prophet knew another way, however, which he summarized in two Hebrew words I've already cited: *dirshuni vi-ḥ'yu* "Seek Me and live" (Amos 5:4). There is no end to the making of books, but no more succinct or profound definition of religion has ever been proposed.

CULTIVATING HOPE

Because the medium through which Scripture suggests human beings might approach God the most effectively is obedience to divine law, it is easy to fall into the trap of thinking of the commandments as a set of obligations. To feel burdened by law, however, is to miss the point entirely . . . and that is the case regardless of whether any specific person does or doesn't find a specific commandment particularly onerous or its observance taxing. Worshiping God may be thought of neither as paying income tax to the Governor of the universe nor as paying rent to the cosmic Landlord who owns the home in which we all live as tenants. Just to the contrary, the worship of God must always be nothing more—or less—than a simple attempt by a human being—or by a group of human beings acting in concert—to create a framework in which that person or those people can elevate what would otherwise remain a vague, inchoate sense that there *might* possibly be a God from the shadowy world of dreamy possibility through the realm of rational and reasonable hope to the domain of faith-based certainty.

In religion, as in every other area of life, unexploited potential is context without content, theoretical possibility without any ultimate grounding in reality. Therefore, as long as people labor under the misconception that the prayers they fail to recite and the worshipful acts they fail to perform constitute examples of unfulfilled needs of the Creator and that, therefore, God is somehow rendered less whole or perfect by their dereliction somewhat in the same way bad debts impact negatively upon the wealth of banks, then their worship of God is really nothing more than an expression of their own self-importance that in the end will only make even stronger their conviction that God exists for their sakes and not *vice versa*.

PRESENCE AND GOVERNANCE

As noted above, there is little, if any, value to keeping the commandments when your personal commitment is rooted solely in the desire to pressure God into behaving in this or that way or doing this or that thing. (And, no, it doesn't matter if you leave that detail regarding your true motivation unexpressed.) On the other hand, the performance of the commandments by someone motivated solely by an unquenchable desire to live a life in God and of God is precisely the kind of worship ordained by Scripture. Furthermore, it is with respect to the faithful whose worship is an extension of their longing for God that the author of the Book of Proverbs wrote, "Know God in every aspect of your life and God will straighten your paths" (Proverbs 3:6)—which is to say: the Almighty will respond to those who exert themselves to know God and to feel the presence—and the governance—of the divine in every aspect of their lives by permitting such people to walk even further along on the path to personal redemption in God and by making straight that path, thus enabling such individuals to move forward expeditiously and efficiently from wherever they are to the goal of their journey, to Jerusalem, city of God.

INVESTED WORSHIP

The three-fold concept that human beings can come to know God by embracing allegiance to the covenant, obedience to the commandments, and purposeful submission to the will of the divine is at the core of Judaism. There is, however, a prerequisite hurdle to clear before embarking on that sacred journey: that the would-be worshiper wholeheartedly embrace the fundamental principle that the commandments of the Torah are empty vessels devoid of any significance other than the meaning which those who perform them invest in them through the sheer force of their will to encounter God within the framework of ritual and rite.

Yes, this places a huge weight on the shoulders of the pilgrim seeking a path forward. But coming to terms with this specific aspect of things is key, even if it is among the most difficult—and disorienting—tasks those who would embrace religion without abandoning their own integrity must face. For some, it might be helpful to think of the commandments of Scripture as words in the language of human spirituality and to focus on the fact that words—the real words of a spoken language—do not exist in real space until a human mouth forms them and propels them for the briefest second into the world of physical existence, and that even then they do not bear any meaning at all other than the meaning their speakers invest in them through their personal identification with the other speakers of that language and their tacit, unwritten, agreement to assign—artificially but usefully—specific sounds to specific things. Similarly, the commandments—the words of the language of religiosity and spirituality—cannot be said to have any real existence until would-be worshipers perform them with the intention of coming closer through their agency to God. And that even then they bear no meaning other than what the performer of the commandment, in tacit agreement with other worshipers, chooses to invest in them.

Therefore, any who are roused to the worship of God by the belief that the commandments possess the magic power to control God's governance of the world are guilty of denying the autonomy of the very God whom Scripture insists exists wholly without reference to the needs, worthy or otherwise, of human worshipers. The underlying principle of all true worship—that submission to the will of God must be a function of the worshiper's longing for communion with the divine realm and not a function of some sort of base, superstitious belief that God's blessings can be provoked automatically through ritual activity—that single principle grants grandeur and nobility to the reverence human beings show God through the performance of worshipful rituals. For Jews, those rituals will always be the commandments of the Torah. But religion really isn't magic. There are no spells, no secret incantations, no lucky charms. All there is, then, is the willing spirit untainted by self-interest and motivated solely by the desire to advance spiritually through the medium of worship to the presence of the living God.

TREMBLING AND DREAD

All who would worship God through fidelity to the commandments and submission to the statutes and laws of Scripture—and, especially, all who yearn to feel the spirit of God palpably and really in their lives—must approach the service of the divine in an atmosphere of awe and trembling tinged with terror and dread, as it is written in the Book of Psalms, "Terror and trembling are come into me / dread has covered me over" (Psalm 55:6), in which verse the awe mentioned denotes extreme reverence in the face of the divine, and the dread and terror reference the natural anxiety any honest worshiper must feel that God might possibly look past the pious motivation behind the worshipful act and focus instead on the hubris that inheres in the concept of worship itself.

The possibility of guileless and selfless worship surely exists. But all who come to the service of God hampered by unproven and unprovable opinions regarding the divine can hardly be said to engaged in meaningful worship at all—and this is true no matter how intensely they might hold those opinions. People, for example, who insist that God will never speak to the faithful in our day and that, as a result, even the most pious individual will never *really* hear the voice of God are guilty of defining the power of God to be limited rather than limitless. Similarly, any who declare to be limited the ability of God to interact totally freely and independently with humanity, or with individual human beings, are guilty of denying the worth both of prayer and of a life of fealty to the commandments, the whole purpose of both of which is to create an opportunity for supplicants to call out to God in word and deed . . . and for God to respond meaningfully and expressively.

Scripture is filled with stories of average people to whom God is depicted as speaking plainly and clearly, and this supposition—that every individual can aspire to hear the voice of God—is at the base of countless biblical passages. The line in the fiftieth psalm, "May God come and not be silent" (Psalm 50:3), may be taken literally, for example, because the poet not only tells us that he called out to God, but also cites the specific oracle he heard in response. Other passages in the Bible are equally explicit. The author of the twentieth psalm, for example, could not have spoken more clearly or unequivocally when asserting that "our divine Sovereign answers us when we call out to him" (Psalm 20:10).

There is no more basic building block in the relationship between God and Israel than the notion that there can be a bridge of understandable language between God and individual men and women. Consequently, all who feel obliged to insist that it is absolutely impossible for contemporaries to hear the voice of God or to learn lessons taught by the Almighty to them alone at the same time that they are not actually able to explain how they know this or even why anyone rational should believe it, such people are guilty of denying a fundamental principle of faith and will eventually deny the concept of divine governance as well—for how can a governor govern without communicating his will to servants possessed of different sets of talents, skills, and abilities? At the very best, they will end up imprisoning the idea that God governs the world behind an impenetrable wall of condition and unlikely possibility they themselves will have built with bricks of arrogance, petulance, and illogic held together by the unvoiced fear that God might deign to speak only to other people and not to them.

STEP BY STEP

The point of worship can never be that God be worshiped, for that would imply that God has needs that can be met—or, impossibly, not met—by human beings anchored to the world. The point of worship, therefore, must always be that worshipers come that much closer to faith through their efforts . . . and to a deep and palpable sense of the presence of God in their lives. For example, the reward for keeping the Sabbath in all the most traditional ways is not that the Sabbath be observed and its regulations and rituals kept, but that Sabbath observers succeed in coming closer to Creator God through the agency of their Sabbath observance. Indeed, the process points to its logical conclusion: observing the Sabbath is not some sort of elaborate contest that Sabbath-observers win when they manage to spend a full day without offending any of the strictures against work that define the day of rest, but rather an opportunity for the faithful to become aware of the presence of God in the world, to become fully sensitive to the relationship between Creator and creation, and to learn to find traces of God in every corner of the created world. This is the most basic meaning of the verse from the seventy-seventh psalm, "Your way was in the sea / Your path, amidst the deep waters. / Will Your footprints then not be seen?" (Psalm 77:20). The question that ends the verse is often taken as a kind of declarative statement to the effect that, despite the fact that God personally parted the waters at the Sea of Reeds, it was nevertheless not possible to perceive any divine footprints in the mud. The more interesting way to read the verse, however, is to take that final line as a rhetorical question and to imagine the poet inviting readers to ask how it could be possible for people who have personally experienced the reality of God's saving grace in the context of their own lives *not* to find traces of the divine in every other corner of the world as well, even in its mud.

In turn, this line of reasoning links the Sabbath to other commandments rooted in the same notion that the Creator may be known through the contemplation—and the safeguarding—of creation. As a result, all who consciously desist from destroying the ecological balance of the world and who refuse to deplete the earth's resources senselessly and irresponsibly—and who *also* seek to honor the Creator by maintaining the rubrics of creation in the traditional ways by *not* sowing their fields with different kinds of grain and by *not* planting their orchards with different kinds of fruit and by *not* wearing garments of linen and wool woven together and by *not* plowing their fields with animals of diverse species under a single yoke—all those who follow these sacred rules and respect the grandeur and very nature of the created world as God made it will come to recognize the presence of God in creation through the respect for the Creator that the commandments they observe will engender in them. That the planet will benefit from their caring approach to the environment is surely so, but what makes these commandments into worshipful acts is the quality they share that enables spiritual advancement in those who observe them faithfully and diligently.

Those individuals are the ones of whom Scripture speaks when it refers to people, male and female, as being created in the image of God (Genesis 1:27). The point of that much-quoted—and much-misquoted—concept is not that people look like God, whatever that would mean, but simply that all who know the Creator through the contemplation of creation will eventually also come to understand that they themselves, by virtue of being part of creation, are stamped with the same indelible traces of the divine that enable all humanity, most definitely including even the *least* educated, *least* cultured, *least* theologically astute individuals, to live in the light of God's enduring presence and both to love God and to feel the light of God's face shining directly into their lives.

AN EMPTY THING . . . FOR YOU

I have returned over and over to the principle that worshipful acts that do not bring worshipers any closer to a sense of God's abiding presence in their lives, even if just infinitesimally so, are by definition not successful acts of divine service at all. Indeed, it is a basic principle that the defining characteristic of *all* the commandments of Scripture is precisely their ability to bring the individuals who accept them and perform them to a level of faith in God that they would otherwise be unable to attain. Therefore, when a specific individual complains that some specific ritual failed to provide sufficient—or any—spiritual gain in that person's spiritual journey toward God, it can be presumed that the shortcoming rests with the person involved and not with the specific commandment under consideration. In classical times, this was the thrust of the famous way Rabbi Mana explained that the deeper meaning of the verse from Deuteronomy, "For it is not an empty thing to you" (Deuteronomy 32:47), has to do with the proper interpretation of the Hebrew word *mikem* ("to you"): if the commandments appear empty to *you*, he taught, then that is surely a result of *your* failure to have studied them sufficiently carefully and to have embraced them with sufficient ardor (Y. Pei·ah 1:1, 3a).

This principle plays itself out again and again in the real worship lives of actual people. For example, of those who build a *sukkah* to dwell in for the seven days of the festival of Sukkot, some are destined to be motivated by the experience only to believe that God watched over the Israelites in the course of their four decades of wandering in the desert, providing for them and making them safe even though they had only makeshift huts in which to dwell and not secure, defensible homes. Others, however, will use the experience of building a *sukkah*—and eating in it and blessing God when they enter it—to come to faith in the core idea that motivates the commandment in the first place: that God can be the ultimate source of security and safety in the lives of all the faithful during the years and decades they wander across the face of the earth and that it is to God, therefore, that they need to feel beholden for the food they eat *and* the water they drink *and* for the shade that protects them from the sun on brutally hot days *and* for the safety they enjoy from the onslaught of wild beasts when they wander alone and unprotected through wild woods filled with predatory animals—which is every day of most people's lives.

Those in the first category—the people who perform the commandment solely, or even principally, as a commemorative act—are obeying the law, but failing to transform the ritual it ordains into an act of true worship capable of ushering them into the presence of God. Their efforts are praiseworthy, but not truly useful. Like young children attempting to help their parents by mimicking their gestures without really understanding what those gestures are supposed to accomplish, such people are not reasonably to be considered sinners or miscreants, just mimics unlikely to accomplish much with their mimicry.

I have referred several times now to the two-word definition of religion pursued with spiritual integrity preserved in the name of the prophet Amos: *dirshuni vi-ḥ'yu* ("seek Me and live"—that is to say, "seek Me and, in so doing, find your way to a life in God"). And the prophet's words are also relevant in this context: the faithful, Amos is suggesting, are not charged with mere obedience to uncountable rules as a kind of test all but the most assiduously dedicated will surely fail, but rather with the *use* of that level of fidelity to sacred law to enable them successfully to seek God's presence in their lives. It is in this sense that the prophet refers to the faithful as being made alive by their faith—not to suggest that those who fail to worship God are not alive, but to say clearly that choosing life—as in the famous commandment, "Choose life so that you and your descendants may live" (Deuteronomy 30:19)—that making that *specific* choice to be fully alive may be accomplished by serving God fully and wholeheartedly, as the very next verse in Deuteronomy makes clear enough by finishing the sentence with the words ."..thus loving the Eternal, your God, by listening to the divine voice and cleaving unto God."

THE TRAPPINGS OF LOVE

Although it is surely true that the foundational idea of worship—at least when undertaken in a Jewish key—is that fidelity to the commandments will bring the worshiper closer to a state of intimacy with Friend God, there is also importance to the fact that Scripture regularly refers to the relationship between God and Israel in terms more suggestive of the relationship between married spouses than merely between friends. This is not solely to encourage the faithful to give themselves totally to God in the manner of two happily married individuals who hold nothing back from each other when they embrace, however, but also to make clear the point that the ideal relationship between the worshiper and God will not solely be about knowledge and will also have all the trappings of human love at its most exalted: intimacy, passion, reciprocity, loyalty, and integrity. The point is that the knowledge of God and the love of God are two sides of the same coin, which truth is demonstrated over and over in Scripture by the regular use of the verb "to know" to denote marital intimacy as opposed to casual acquaintanceship, as for example in the verse "And Adam knew his wife and she conceived and then gave birth to Cain" (Genesis 4:1).

WORSHIP AS THE ANTIDOTE TO MELANCHOLY

Although it is not unreasonable to imagine God as the cosmic version of a medieval lord on whose huge estate all the earth's people live out their lives, it is nevertheless self-defeating to approach worship depressed by the feelings of obligation, debt, and responsibility that surely must have typified the mindset of serfs who spent the days of their lives tilling other people's fields. One of the great insights of Scripture, in fact, is that God not only *may*, but actually *must*, be worshiped in gladness and joy by people imbued with a deep, unquenchable desire to serve God with all their hearts and with all their souls. The effort to evoke that specific set of emotions, therefore, is crucial to the cultivation of a life of the spirit that leads to the knowledge of God.

For this reason, success in overcoming the natural melancholy any who live in the world must feel when they contemplate the vagaries and vicissitudes of human life—and in replacing that sense of unhappiness with joy rooted in submission to God—is such an important goal to attempt to attain that the very presence of God on earth can reasonably be said to depend on the collective success of humanity in this specific regard, as the prophet Zachariah said in God's name: "Rejoice and exult, O daughter of Zion, for thus shall I come to dwell in your midst, says God" (Zachariah 2:14).

Similar lessons appear throughout Scripture. The prophet Ezekiel, for example, learned as much when God commanded him to write out a scroll filled with sad elegy and bitter lament. He did as commanded, but when God commanded him to "eat the scroll" (Ezekiel 3:1), and he did eat it, he found it as sweet as honey and not bitter at all. With this, the prophet teaches his readers a profound lesson: that all who would listen carefully to even the most dour words of God—and internalize them no less totally than if they actually *had* ingested them—will find the experience sweet and not at all bitter.

NIGHTTIME

Although it is true that worship may be undertaken at any hour of the day or night, it is also the case that nighttime is the *ideal* time for pursuing the worship of God through the medium of study, which lesson was taught in ancient times by Rabbi Simon Ḥasida with reference to the lyre that hung directly over King David's bed. When midnight came, Rabbi Simon taught, a northern breeze would enter the king's bedchamber and vibrate the lyre's strings strongly enough to wake the slumbering king, who would then rise immediately from his bed and immerse himself in the study of Torah until dawn. (This legend may be found in two different Talmudic tractates, at B. Berakhot 50b and at B. Sanhedrin 16a.)

The explanation of the notion that nighttime is especially conducive to worshipful study, and to worship in general, does not rest in historical details about the past, however. Rather, the connection is to be explained with reference to the nature of nighttime itself, for night is the traditional time for the expression of longing and yearning for God, as the psalmists wrote, "At midnight, I rise to acclaim You because of the justice of Your laws" (Psalm 119: 62) and "I recall You while in bed / I think of You during the watches of night" (Psalm 63:7). Nor is this a feature solely of days gone by: those who rise from their beds in the middle of the night even in our own day to seek the palpable presence of God may expect to be blessed by God for their efforts, just as a different psalmist began his poem with the words "Bless ye God, all servants of God who stand in the House of God at night" (Psalm 134:1), and continues to say "God, Maker of heaven and earth, will bless you from Zion" (134:3)—and who in our Temple-less world can more reasonably feel that they nevertheless live in the House of God than those who immerse themselves in the study of the books between the lines of which God's word dwells in our midst?

Moderns tend to work during the day and sleep at night. But nighttime is the time of darkness. And darkness itself, which is *defined* as the absence of light yet which *feels* as though it exists nonetheless as a thing unto itself, is the perfect medium in which to encounter a God who exists no less absolutely than impossibly in a world that cannot contain even the shadow of divinity but which nonetheless somehow does . . . or occasionally feels like it does.

STONES ON A PATH

There is a natural distinction to be drawn between worshipful acts that are difficult, costly, time-consuming, and physically arduous and those that are none, or only some, of those things. It is, therefore, incumbent upon the faithful to keep in mind at all times that the only distinction of importance between the various commandments of Scripture has to do neither with the degree to which it is arduous to perform them nor with the amount of money it costs to undertake them, but rather solely with the degree to which they lend themselves to being invested with inner yearning for God and for the presence of God.

One way to conceptualize this idea would be to think of the commandments as steppingstones along an endless path that leads to the divine throne room in which God sits in sacred splendor amidst the angels and cherubs. Some of the stones may be large and others small, some may be fashioned of costly alabaster and others of cement or mud, some may be aesthetically hewn and others merely utilitarian . . . but, in the end, the only real purpose any has is briefly to support the weight of pilgrims seeking their personal paths to Jerusalem, thus making it possible for them to make progress in their journeys by stepping across to the next stone on the path.

When the ancient teacher, Ben Azzai, taught the lesson cited above to the effect that the reason you should hurry to perform simple precepts with no less zeal than you bring to those deemed difficult or important is because "one commandment will inevitably lead to another" (M. Avot 4:2), this is exactly what he meant. And this image of the commandments as steppingstones on a path is also the basis for the famous lesson of Rabbi Judah the Patriarch exhorting his listeners to be "no less scrupulous in the performance of the simplest commandment than in the performance of the most difficult" (M. Avot 2:1).

In the end, though, no one collects steppingstones as a hobby. No one wants to see them in a museum. Nor does anyone really want to admire the stones that constitute someone else's path. You don't think much about them at all, in fact—until you begin a journey across a muddy field and then suddenly become aware that you can only move forward efficiently—or at all—by stepping on the stones someone has conveniently provided along the path you hoped to take, thus allowing you to progress without sinking into the mud. Of course, that is not *precisely* true: you could pause in your journey and remain immobile until you find the wherewithal to manufacture your own steppingstones. But since you are the traveler and the journey is your own, what virtue could there possibly be in insisting on making no progress on your journey by refusing to stepping on steppingstones already in place along the path you wish to follow?

NOT ATOP THE LADDER

If God appeared to Jacob as he lay on the ground asleep at Bethel to bring him comfort and reassurance, then it follows that the vision vouchsafed to him that very evening of a ladder leading from earth to heaven with angels ascending and descending its rungs was meant to teach a lesson relating to the long and lonely road that lay before him and thereby to encourage him to think of the journey he was on positively even before actually setting forth in earnest. But what *was* that lesson? Different readers will think of different answers, but mine is that the lesson had to do with the service of God to which Jacob was being called and was that divine service is not an all-or-nothing proposition, that the commandments that define that service are best thought of as rungs on a personal ladder that one ascends one by one on the journey from childhood through adolescence to spiritual and emotional adulthood, that the journey is thus in many ways its own destination. Surely that image can function as a satisfying model for spiritual growth for many . . . as long as they recall that the ladder cannot exist in reality because God exists outside of both space and time, and that the notion of ascending to God's sacred throne room in the divine palace in the sky only works for people who understand that there is no throne . . . and no palace. (The sky does exist, of course. But surely that's not the point!)

EMPTY CRATES

The commandments of Scripture are empty crates the sole worth of which derives from whatever importance the faithful are able to invest in them as part of the ongoing effort to encounter God in the context of divine worship. Indeed, the fact that it is possible to succeed at investing the commandments with enough personal energy to transform them into private, idiosyncratic, totally worshiper-specific acts of fealty and devotion is what makes it feasible to seek God through the medium of formal ritual in the first place. For this reason, the old dictum of the Talmudic sage Rav to the effect that there is at least some merit in the performance of a commandment even absent intentionality must be supposed to mean that there is always the chance that mere exposure to the commandments will inspire the listless worshiper *eventually* to undertake real worship. On the other hand, interpreting Rav's remark to mean that form without content in the context of worship will be good enough for most will lead the would-be worshiper off in precisely the wrong direction.

DISTINCT GROUPS UNDER THE LAW

A basic principle of faith is that the distinctions Scripture makes between classes of people in terms of which commandments they are obliged to observe are not intended to elevate one group in society over another or to make one more sacred than another (or, even less likely, to suggest that one is more special or more beloved in the eyes of God than some other), but merely to suggest an idea about God that can be embraced by the contemplation of some specific distinction between diverse groups within society.

Therefore, the commandments specifically linked to the Land of Israel are not presented in Scripture to suggest that those who live in the Holy Land are more capable than anyone else of loving God or cleaving unto God, but rather to signal that God, who is the moral core of being in the physical world, can be approached through the various ways Scripture suggests humans might successfully venerate the Holy Land, the territory considered by the authors of Scripture to exist at very center of Creation and thus to be the place on earth the most suffused with God's creative presence. These commandments will obviously feel different to residents of the Land of Israel who can observe these commandments and to diasporan types who can only contemplate them, but the goal—namely the privilege of stepping one small step closer toward God through the medium of the specific commandment under consideration—will be the same for both groups. The same can be asserted for the different groups of commandments intended for priests and non-priests, for firstborns and their younger siblings, and for men and women: all have at their core *not* any desire on the part of Scripture to enfranchise one group at the expense of another, but simply to suggest that the contemplation of the specific ways in which different groups within society take the specifics of their personal circumstances into account as they chart their different spiritual journeys forward can provide spiritual insight for people who themselves do not belong to that category of individual. Nor is it likely accidental that the system more or less guarantees that no two worshipers will have exactly the same set of ritual requirements to fulfill. In turn, this detail suggests yet another a great truth: that, in the end, none can travel to God along another's path, just as all worshipers will have their own sets of wishes and hopes for the future propelling them forward. Indeed, the great paradox at the heart of the matter is that precisely what makes all pilgrims on their way to Jerusalem into each other's spiritual partners is the distinctiveness each brings to the journey. That thought will possibly puzzle outsiders looking in from afar, but will seem obvious to people on their personal journeys to the Holy City in the company of uncountable others making the same pilgrimage to the same place without taking precisely the same path forward.

SERVANTS OF GOD

There are those whose efforts to perform the commandments of the Torah aesthetically or artistically enhance the spiritual worth of their worship because their efforts lead them to a new level of intimacy with the God described in Scripture as embodying the quintessence of beauty, as we read in the Song of Songs, "Beloved, Thou art loveliness itself" (Song of Songs 1:16). As a result, any effort to acquire splendid ritual appurtenances that is fueled by the desire to know God as the ultimate source of beauty and aesthetic perfection in the world is praiseworthy, as a very wealthy king once advised us all to "honor God with [our] wealth" (Proverbs 3:9). However, regarding all those people who purchase all the most expensive accouterments of religious ritual solely for the sake of vaunting themselves over worshipers less able to afford such extravagant expenditures, that same king warned that "wealth will serve no purpose in a day of wrath" (Proverbs 11:4). And, indeed, such people only succeed at distancing themselves from God and making of their own self-importance a kind of impenetrable barrier between themselves and God.

PLEASURE AND WORSHIP

It is essential that an individual seek God not merely in the context of intellectual, emotional, or spiritual satisfaction, but also imbued with the sense of the sensual pleasure that comes from seeking God in the context of love. The poet whose poem is the longest and most detailed in the Book of Psalms, for example, returns to this theme again and again: "I take great pleasure in Your commandments, which I love" (Psalm 119:47), "I take pleasure in Your laws / I do not forget Your word" (Psalm 119:16), "My pleasure lies in Your commandments" (Psalm 119:143).

The basic concept is simply that, just as God exists in the real world *not* merely as a philosophical construct in the world of ideas but as part of perceptible reality, so must the commandments—the acts of worship that collectively form a bridge between the created world and Creator God—take on sensory and sensual reality in the lives of the faithful. Indeed, this experience of feeling God to be present not simply within the confines of your private intellectual universe, but as a physically real presence in your personal space is the threshold experience that transforms speculative, tentative belief in the efficacy of worship as a bridge to God into wholehearted faith.

Therefore, although it is true that those who view the commandments as jobs to do and as obligations to address cannot be said to accomplish much with their begrudging worship, it is also the case that people whose observance leads solely to intellectual satisfaction and not to sensory pleasure in the experience of God's presence made palpable and real by that worship have also seriously missed the boat.

A KIND OF BRIDGE

The acts of worship that the faithful undertake do not only serve collectively as a bridge between them and God, but also as a kind of profound bond that links them to each other . . . and, indeed, to all in the world who seek to know God through the medium of submission to divine law. Among Jews, this is especially true: the commonality of worship and the use of a single, universal language of prayer links not only Jews in every place to each other, but also and especially the Jews of the Diaspora to the Jews of Israel who, having no need to be gathered in from exile, are by their very situation one step closer to redemption than their diasporan brethren. In turn, developing and sustaining this sense of oneness and unity—to the extent that it suggests the unity of God—is itself an act of worship worth cultivating. But this is not *solely* an inner-Jewish phenomenon: it is also the golden cord that binds together the faithful of every nation and ethnicity who seek spiritual perfection through loyalty and submission to God.

Chapter Six

The Sixth Gate

Obeying God

The world is filled to overflowing with people vying with each other to express their devotion to the sanctity and ineffable holiness of Scripture in the most extravagant, flowery language possible. But only a small percentage of those people feel bidden actually to take the laws laid down therein seriously and to obey them even at all, let alone with strict attention to their most picayune detail. Like children who like the *concept* of having parents who care for them and nurture them but who balk at following the rules and regulations their parents lay down as the *context* in which all that nurturing and caring can actually take place, such people speak lovingly and approvingly of the *concept* of divine law without feeling personally called to observance.

    Yet, for all the concept may be seriously off-putting for some, the whole concept that God may be sought—and the divine presence made palpably real in the actual lives of regular people—through the medium of submission to law rests on the assumption that those laws exist not merely to be contemplated or elaborated through legal discourse and debate, but actually to be obeyed strictly and carefully. Indeed, to celebrate "the law" without feeling concomitantly obliged to observe the actual laws that constitute "the law" is not just illogical, but also utterly counterproductive: from the point of view of spiritual physics, it is precisely from the tension between wishing *both* to live fully autonomously *and* fully to submit to the will of God that derives the energy that can propel individuals a step or two further on the road to spiritual fulfillment. To speak in specifically Jewish terms, professing endless devotion to the Torah but feeling free to remain unobservant of its laws and statutes is neither how the system is supposed to work nor how it actually does work. Missing that point, therefore—and, consequently, becoming mired in the peculiar notion that spiritual energy need not be generated at all, and certainly not in the way all usable energy is generated in the physical universe through tension, friction, conflict, and opposition—is to overlook the fact that the spiritual system proposed by Scripture works in the first place by harnessing the energy that comes from reining in the animal instincts that characterize human life at its least noble and using the resultant tension to propel reluctant pilgrims one step closer toward their finer angels, toward redemption, toward God.

For the citizens of free republics, there will inevitably be something suspect about questioning the right of any individual to live a life unfettered by allegiance to rules other than the actual laws of the land. That may well be the case as a principle of political science, but surely—and even in the most free society—the individual has an inalienable right to suppress any specific desire or inclination as part of an ongoing effort to find God in the world through the medium of personal submission to divine law. And that too is a wholly embraceable principle of political science!

THE GREAT RIDDLE

Although the function of law in the context of divine revelation is to create an opportunity to pursue the veneration of God within the framework of daily life, it is the special insight of Scripture that those same laws can also open the door to the perception of God as a fully present force for good in the world. Therefore, those who evaluate those laws with reference to the specific degree of likelihood that they themselves would have enacted similar laws and statues if they had somehow been charged by the peoples of the world with becoming the planet's supreme legislators have misunderstood the reason for which Scripture routes the path toward redemption through obedience, fealty, and submission in the first place. The essential concept of the Torah is to use different kinds of laws and statutes to lower—and eventually even perhaps totally to remove—the almost (but *only* almost) impenetrable barrier that separates humankind from God, a wall fashioned from the feeling human beings can cultivate all too easily that, somehow, it is they who rule over the world in which they live rather than God who rules over it and, by extension, over them as well.

There is paradox afoot here too, however. Indeed, undertaking a journey without movement to a God who does not and cannot exist in any particular place that is undertaken by obeying laws and statutes that are presented in Scripture as being reflective of the will of a God who is also described as a perfect Being who can therefore know neither need nor lack and who, therefore, cannot reasonably to be imagined to *want* anything at all—agreeing to set forward on such a journey is the beginning of unraveling the great challenge that rests at the core of the decision to pursue the knowledge of God through the medium of obedience to the commandments of the Torah.

WHAT TO TAKE ALONG

Seeking communion with the divine realm through the medium of submission to law is the traditional Jewish way to approach God. Nevertheless, those who seek to travel this path will only succeed in their journey if they remember to bring certain indispensable tools along with them:

- a hammer strong enough to pulverize any preconceived notion of what God's true nature must be like,
- a knife sharp enough to shred everything ever written about God that an individual might be inclined to substitute for faith acquired through personal experience of the divine,
- a shovel with which to bury every book in which it is written that an individual can come to know God by following someone else's spiritual path . . . and also every book in which readers are encouraged to believe that the moral strength and spiritual creativity necessary to pave a personal path forward toward redemption in God merely by wishing for it inheres in the human condition and is therefore available to people merely because they *are* human beings, and
- a mirror, so as to see the image of God stamped on their own faces a moment before they despair utterly of ever finding God and decide to turn back and abandon the journey entirely.

THE CRUX OF THE MATTER

Every commandment has an outer aspect, which consists of an overt halakhic ritual and an interior aspect that serves as the inner kernel of meaning embedded in the physical deed that constitutes the performance of that commandment.

The outer aspect of the commandment to recite the Shema Yisrael prayer morning and evening, for example, consists of the actual recitation of the words of the prayer twice daily, while the inner aspect has to do with accepting that God is one and the name of God is one and that God is the sole example of absolute, undifferentiated unity that exists or that ever could exist in the world. These two aspects are clearly related, but they differ dramatically in terms of doability. Coming to faith in the unity of God requires decades of meditative effort and intellectual endeavor. Learning the recite the words of the Shema, on the other hand, will take most people no more than a few minutes.

The upshot of all this is that, while learning to recite the Shema is something that children can do easily, the act of investing the outer shape of the commandment with its inner essence—which is its heart and its soul in every real sense of the word—is the work of a lifetime of concentrated spiritual effort. It is neither simple nor easy. More to the slightly depressing point, it is more than possible to devote serious energy to its accomplishment without *ever* really succeeding. (The fact that we spend so much energy insisting, especially to children, that precisely the opposite is the case has a good deal more to do with the way moderns tend to think about religion than with religion itself.) Indeed, it is telling just how reasonable it feels to hope that there could be real spiritual advancement even through the unsuccessful effort to perform a commandment properly, a notion that is as illogical as it is unlikely. And yet, in its own way, just that fantasy lives at the heart of the religious enterprise for a remarkable number of people. As a result, stepping away from it—wholly and without ambivalence or regret—is the first real step on the journey to Jerusalem most of us can take.

WITH ALL YOUR HEART

The point of Sabbath observance is not to provide a context in which the human need for periodic rest can be satisfied after a tiresome and burdensome week of work. The point of the dietary laws is not to provide a context in which human beings can eat healthy, fortifying foods at the same time they learn to avoid foodstuffs that could potentially harm them. The point of the observance of the festivals of Israel is not to provide a context in which people can formally recall certain specific events that happened in the past to the ancestors of the Jewish people.

It is, in fact, *never* necessary to rationalize the observance of the commandments with reference to any human need or desire other than the human need *and* desire to create a context in which the worship of God becomes possible. Moreover, this way of God-focused worship is the way of pure faith regarding which the prophet Isaiah wrote, "this is the way—veer neither to the right or the left" (Isaiah 30:21). There is, however, a peculiarity in the text of Isaiah well worth considering in this regard: the word for "veer not to the right," which ought to be written with the Hebrew letter *yod* as its second letter, has an *aleph* there instead, thereby creating a word related in form, if not in formal meaning, to the word for faith, *emunah*, which is written with three of the same letters. And what did the prophet mean by spelling the word with an *aleph* instead of with a *yod,* if not to identify the path toward which he was pointing as the way of faith along which members of the covenanted community who believe in God should spend their lives wandering without veering off from it in any other direction at all?

There is also another way, the one called in the thirty-seventh psalm (and other places in Scripture) "the not-good-way," and this is the way of worshipers who take great pride in the level of their commitment to the commandments of the Torah, but who, missing the point entirely, end up using that commitment as part of an elaborate campaign to win the admiration of the world and to establish their personal places in it. Directly to people in this category Rabbi Zadok addressed the injunction to "make the Torah neither a crown designed to garner you the veneration of others nor a shovel to dig with" (M. Avot 4:7). And in the Torah itself, we read, "Do not make anything into an idol" (Exodus 20:4 and Deuteronomy 5:8), which is to say: nothing at all, not even the words "Do not make anything into an idol" or the book that contains them.

STRINGENCY

There is no need whatsoever to adopt a fundamentalist/literalist approach to Scripture to justify the decision to live a life of strict fidelity to the law. On the other hand, any who live lives of rigorous loyalty to religious law because of an overwhelming desire to transform the commandments of the Torah from empty vessels possessed solely of *potential* spiritual importance into useful paving tools with which it might be possible *actually* to create a path to God—that kind of legal stringency is totally reasonable and logical, and requires no secondary justification at all.

In our peculiar world, though, strict adherence to legal detail is considered a natural bedfellow of fundamentalism. Indeed, appearing to be possessed of total spiritual integrity—and thus widely to be taken as someone who refuses to insist on the knowability of things that none may or does know with certainty—and nevertheless remaining strictly observant of the rites and rituals that characterize traditional religious behavior seems to strike most moderns as a sign of spiritual schizophrenia. But just the opposite is actually the case, and the moment most of us begin to live lives of total spiritual integrity is precisely when we finally abandon the unjustifiable notion that submission to the will of God will only make real sense in the context of a fundamentalist worldview.

In the end, strict adherence to the minutiae of the law for the sake of more fully knowing God through the medium of fealty, obedience, and submission is not only praiseworthy, but intensely so. Nor is it irrelevant to note that the fantasy that the religious individual must necessarily make a choice between total intellectual honesty and strict religious observance is mostly just the self-serving fantasy of people eager to feel good about living lives characterized by a lackadaisical approach to divine law. But there is no real choice between the two, nor—speaking realistically—could there ever be: knowing God requires that the would-be person of faith embrace guileless integrity while at the same time also engaging with the mountain of details that the careful, thoughtful fulfillment of each of God's commandments naturally entails.

Mythology and history are discrete kingdoms separated by a slightly porous border. Therefore, any who feel unable to justify their strict-constructionist approach to tradition and law other than with reference to the *identity* of history and mythology deprive their own worship of anything more than perfunctory meaning. The bottom line is that there is only one way to evaluate religious observance and that is with respect to the degree to which it does or does not bring the worshiper closer to feeling the perceptible presence of God in his or her personal space. In ancient times, this was the truth the author of the ninety-sixth psalm wished to teach his readers by instructing them to "bring [their] gifts and come to the Temple courtyards" (Psalm 96:8). Take your gifts, the poet is saying, and bring them to the innermost courtyard of the House of God, that chamber of the human heart in which God may always be found by those who seek the divine presence in a state of purity and absolute honesty, of candor untainted with arrogance or egotism, and of uncompromising spiritual integrity. If you cannot find your way to that place, then you will be unable to offer your gifts to anyone at all, let alone to God. (The modern version would be the image of the hapless invitee to a fancy dinner party who purchases a lovely gift to bring to the party's hosts, but then loses the slip of paper on which he had written down their address. The gift retains its value . . . but only theoretically and not at all practically.)

STONES OF REALIZED HOPE

The most basic of all scriptural notions regarding the nature of divinity is that God exists far beyond the ken of even those men and women who seek communion with the divine realm the most ardently and with the most passion and dedication. Yet it is the special insight of Scripture that God, somehow, may be known nonetheless—or at least perceived for a fleeting moment or two in the course of a lifetime—through the medium of submission to divine law in the context of absolute honesty and integrity. To lie about the nature of these laws, therefore, is the equivalent of disabling them, thus intentionally depriving them of their usefulness and validity. And this is so, of course, even if the lies themselves are flattering.

Exploiting the laws and commandments of Scripture for personal gain is thus abandoning the sole road the leads to Jerusalem, to God. On the other hand, the proper use of the commandments is endorsed by Scripture as the equivalent of paving a path toward communion with God with stones of realized hope. (The hope, of course, is that those faithful souls paving the path might possibly find the strength of character *and* the spiritual integrity to wander the path toward redemption without being distracted by siren lies, or by egotism or arrogance, or by the disapproval—or, even more distractingly, by the approval—of others.)

Scripture endorses this idea over and over in a wide variety of contexts. For instance, the famous commandment to love God "with all your heart and with all your soul and with all your might" (Deuteronomy 6:5) is followed *not* with pious exhortations to wait patiently until you are visited by an angel bearing the gift of transcendent personal salvation, but with practical, useful suggestions for seeking God in the context of daily life. Nor is there any indication that people who seek to use these precepts to invite God's palpable presence into their personal lives—that is, those who keep the words of Torah alive in their own hearts *and* who teach them diligently to their children *and* who speak of them at home and while they are away from home on long journeys *and* who bind them on their arms *and* who place them firmly between their eyes *and* who write them on the doorposts of their homes *and* who engrave them on the gates of their cities—there is no indication whatsoever that these people are behaving basely or poorly by attempting to create a context in which they will possibly come to know—or at least to know *of—the* unknowable God. Just to the contrary, by obeying the commandments—and by using them to pave a path forward toward the kind of spiritual wholeness that leads to the possibility of salvation in God—they are adding to their sanctity and using them for the purpose for which they were surely intended to be used all along.

The rabbis of ancient times were unambiguously hostile to the notion of using obedience to the laws of Scripture for an individual's own ends, Indeed, Hillel's ancient, uncompromising dictum preserved twice in the Mishnah (at M. Avot 1:13 and 4:7) to the effect that even casual use of the crown—he meant the crown of Torah—should be punished with death is merely the extreme expression of this idea. The use of the commandments of the Bible to forge a covenantal relationship between the individual keeping them and the God perceived to be their divine Author, however, is not negatively evaluated as an act of exploitation at all, but rather as the realization and actualization of Scripture's most sacred program: the transformation of the merely human into the expressly sacred, the transformation of the mundane realm of ordinary men and women into the kingdom of God on earth.

Chapter 6
VARIEGATION

As already noted, the essential idea of Scripture is that communion with the living God may be sought by human beings through the medium of mindful submission to law. And then, to practicalize this possibility, Scripture proceeds to offer its readers a wide range of commandments, laws, statutes, and ritual edicts, each designed to escort the seeker one step closer to God along the path of obedience and fealty.

These commandments may be divided down into a large number of different categories according to their essential natures and details: positive and negative commandments, commandments based on a recurring calendar of obligation and commandments that devolve upon the faithful in a more haphazard way, commandments specifically designated for those who live in the Holy Land and commandments unrelated to an individual's specific place of residence, commandments tied to special events in the lives of the faithful—their weddings or the births of their children or the deaths of their parents—and commandments that bear no such relationship to the events of human life, commandments specifically designated for observance by men and commandments that relate specifically to women, commandments that will only be feasible for the wealthy to observe and commandments given to all without regard for social class, commandments that pertain to relations between people and commandments specifically pertaining to the relationship between an individual and God, commandments given especially to members of the House of Israel and commandments designated for all humanity, commandments that apply solely to certain professions and commandments unrelated to the way someone earns a living, commandments that may only be carried out in the Temple in Jerusalem and commandments doable in any time and any place, and commandments that are specifically applicable to the descendants of Aaron the High Priest and commandments intended for all without regard for sacerdotal rank or status.

There is a deep spiritual point to this variegation of commandment and statute. Although Scripture holds out the democratic idea of equality under the law as a necessary—and desirable—basis for the fair functioning of society when it declares that "one Torah shall apply to the citizen and the stranger living among you" (Exodus 12:49), the reality of the system is that the divine service to which any specific individual is called will never mirror the service to which another is called exactly.

In turn, this specific notion—that the existence of one covenant for all does not imply that all members of the covenanted community will be redeemed through allegiance to precisely the same set of laws—is the precise parallel of the concept that all men and women are created in God's image. The Torah says as much unequivocally several times in the opening chapters of the Bible, but does not scruple to explain how all human beings can be made in God's image if there are no two people in the world who resemble each other precisely. Other than in the case of identical twins (and not even *always* in that case once they are grown), no two people are each other's mirror image. Yet all are created in the image of God. Similarly, no two people bear precisely the same obligations under the terms of the covenant, yet all are included in the great covenantal idea that redemption may be sought—and achieved—through fidelity to the same set of divine laws.

PARTNERS IN CREATION

God does not simply materialize in the world through the performance of the commandments, but materializes according to the givens of the commandment being performed at any given moment in the creative consciousness of the specific individual undertaking to fulfill it—and it is in this sense that the ancients described God as a potential partner in dialogue and relationship. In the biblical corpus, this is the notion that underlies those passages in Scripture that refer to God being the God of a specific individual, as, for example, at 2 Samuel 7:14 or 1 Chronicles 17:13 or 28:6, where it is said that King Solomon, by building the Temple in Jerusalem, became the child of God—which passages certainly do not mean to imply that the king somehow magically became the real child of God, whatever that would mean, but rather that his relationship to God was henceforth to be so personal, so private, and so fully and unambiguously idiosyncratic that it would come to resemble the relationship between parents and their children, relationships that, for all they may share certain similarities from family to family, are nonetheless totally specific to the members of each separate family group.

It is also in this context that we can understand the various verses in Scripture that suggest that the commandments are a kind of song that worshipers sing with their bodies and spirits, with their ritual activities and their prayers. When, for example, we read the poet's simple statement in the 119th psalm that, "For me, Your laws are the songs I sing in my dwelling house" (Psalm 119:54), the point is that the poet has come to see his body as the earthly home of his soul and that it is through the use of ritual that the poet has managed to transcend mere theorizing and actually to worship God through the medium of law in that home. In other passages, however, it is the entire Torah that is called a song and not just the laws presented in it. These verses, however, have the same idea embedded in them: just as a song does not truly exist in the world until an individual sings it in the presence of someone capable of hearing and deciphering its melody and cadences, so does divine law merely exist in the realm of conceptual ideas until human beings devoted to the worship of God find the spiritual strength to usher it into the domain of active reality through the sheer force of their collective will to know God through the medium of fidelity and submission to law.

In this context, we could even say that mindful worshipers actually liberate the commandments from their literary prison in Scripture and grant them the freedom to exist in the world unfettered by etymology, morphology, phonology, lexicography, or grammar. This, in fact, is the way worshipers can become the partners of God in the cause of cosmic redemption: just as God redeems the faithful from physicality and human mortality, so do sincere worshipers redeem the commandments from their literary prison and grant them the freedom to exist in the world.

This is not a new idea. Indeed, it was taught millennia ago by Rabbi Aḥa bar Yaakov, who based himself on the verse from Exodus in which it is noted that the Ten Commandments were written "with writing that was the writing of God engraved on the tablets (Exodus 32:16). Playing on the assonance of the Hebrew words for "engraved" (ḥarut) and "freedom" (ḥeirut), Rabbi Aḥa taught the great paradox that inheres in the concept of worship: that the commandments themselves are capable of acting as agents of redemption for those who, by translating them from theory to deed, redeem them by making them real in space and time and so enable them to function in the world as agents of redemption for those who embrace them and who, in a manner of speaking, redeem them.

EMBRACING THE CORE

The first step in any attempt to worship God through the medium of submission to divine law is to pierce through the outer layer of ritual action to the idea that rests at the core of the commandment. Then, after identifying that idea, the second goal becomes to embrace that *specific* idea through the performance of that *specific* commandment, thereby translating it from the domain of language into the physically real context in which normal human beings can make progress toward achieving communion with God.

This effort to identify and embrace the core ideas about God presented in Scripture by fulfilling the commandments rests at the center of all Jewish religious life; it is the catalytic agent that transforms ritual from superstition to noble effort, from mere magic to a path capable of leading those who walk along it to the presence of the living God. For example, the Torah tells the story of the exodus from Egypt at great length not solely so that the latter-day descendants of those people liberated from bondage to Pharaoh can know about the various events that befell their ancestors as they sought their freedom, but rather so that the descendants of those people might be moved to accept the concept that God functions in the world even today as the source of liberation for all, both those held in place by real chains and those held back in life by chains fashioned of their own moral inconsistencies, inadequacies, shortcomings, and flaws. In this way, the scriptural narrative and the laws that develop out of it unite in the hearts of the faithful to create a path along which individuals may travel forward toward the great goal of living life in the presence of God.

COUNTING THE COMMANDMENTS

The peculiar notion that God may be accessed through simple, faithful obedience to a finite set divine laws in the same way a program on a computer may be accessed by someone who masters some finite set of specific keystrokes is negated by the fact that no one has ever actually succeeded in conclusively counting the commandments of the Torah. Indeed, although a list of those who have attempted to compose a detailed enumeration of the commandments reads like a roster of the greatest sages of talmudic and post-talmudic Judaism, the fact remains that none of them managed to produce a list that was universally accepted as authoritative.

This maddening quality of the law—that its codicils cannot be counted or named conclusively, yet must be obeyed unconditionally—is reflective of the nature of blessing in general. Indeed, it is the opinion of many that it is precisely *because* the laws of Scripture serve collectively as a blessing for humankind that they cannot be counted conclusively. Numerous texts from antiquity speak directly to this point. Abraham's descendants, Scripture says, will also resist precise counting, as is made clear in God's promise to Abraham to make his "progeny as the dust of the earth such that they will only be countable by someone who can also count the world's specks of dust" (Genesis 13:16). Indeed, Scripture specifically ordains that any attempt to conduct a census in Israel must have its negative consequences vitiated in advance, as is evident from the text at Exodus 30:12, which decrees that a census of the Israelites be taken by eliciting half-shekel donations from the people to be enumerated and then counting the coins instead of the people. In that specific way, the text implies, the nation will avoid the plague that would otherwise ensue from counting the people one by one in the obvious way. And the same point is made when Scripture lists the dire consequences that actually did ensue when King David ill-advisedly chose to conduct a census in the normal way, as related at length in 2 Samuel 24.

In later times, the rabbis relied on the same assumptions about the nature of blessing when they noted that "blessing may never be found in the weighed, measured or counted thing, but only in something the specific dimensions and weight of which are hidden from the eye (B. Taanit 8b and Bava Metzia 42a).

On the other hand, the famous *midrash* of Rabbi Simlai preserved in the Talmud (at B. Makkot 23b) according to which there are precisely 613 commandments in Scripture, only serves to underscore the underlying principle that the commandments may never be counted: their number may well have been known to Rabbi Simlai, but even *he* did not attempt to produce an authoritative list of them. And the chances are strong that even Rabbi Simlai didn't mean his number to be taken literally anyway and that 613 was taken symbolically as the sum of the days of the solar year (which is said to match the number of negative commandments) and the number of discrete limbs and organs in the human body (which is said to match the number of positive commandments). This, in turn, was probably intended to suggest that individuals truly in search of God through the medium of submission to divine law will devote themselves, body and soul, to the task every day of their earthly lives.

True, this interpretation seems to be contradicted by the teaching of Rabbi Hamnuna preserved slightly further along in the Talmud (at B. Makkot 23b–24a) to the effect that the number 613 is derived from the fact that the numerological value of the Hebrew word *torah* is 611. The number 611 would then represent the number of commandments revealed through Moses to the people, while the remaining two would be those that the Israelites camped at the foot of Mount Sinai would have heard, so Rabbi Hamnuna, directly from God. Rabbi Hamnuna's *midrash* is clever, but surely Naḥmanides was right to label it a mere *asmakhta*, that is: an inspiring, interesting lesson unrelated to the actual literary history of Scripture *or* its laws.

Given the long history of efforts to count the commandments, however, it seems wrong to conclude that there is no point to the effort. There is *indeed* a point, only one not predicated on the doability of the task at hand: the commandments that can and cannot be counted are the perfect path along which the righteous might stumble forward toward a God who exists in the world and who cannot exist in the world, that God whom human beings can know and who is so totally unknowable as reasonably to have been acclaimed by the prophet (at Isaiah 45:15) as the Hidden God and for King Solomon to have described as being ever enshrouded in impermeable mist and opaque fog, which is to say: in an impenetrable cloud of unknowing.

In turn, the image of a God who may not be perceived being served by commandments that cannot be counted is meant to point directly to a deep truth: that the journey to God may be undertaken but never actually completed, that revelation is poetry not prose, music not science, yearning not consummation, desire not the fulfillment of desire. And, indeed, the pilgrims of ancient times journeyed to Jerusalem and entered the city through its gates and the Temple Mount through its several portals. But no pilgrim was permitted to enter into the Holy of Holies, for theirs was travel *toward* rather than travel *to*, an asymptotical journey to a destination that can be approached but never quite fully attained.

ALACRITY

In religion, as in most things, attitude counts. And, indeed, one of the best indications of sincerity in worship untainted by self-serving egotism is precisely the enthusiasm an individual brings to worship. Indeed, it is the overt willingness to be obedient to the strictures of the commandments—and the delight that that obedience engenders—that are jointly behind those passages in Scripture that refer to the relationship between human beings and God both as though it were parallel to the relationship between servants and their masters and mistresses, and *also* as though it were parallel to the relationship between earthly lovers.

This ability to use alacrity to demonstrate the depth of someone's desire to know God through the medium of observance is behind an old *midrash* on the verse from Exodus "You shall keep the *matzot*" (that is: the commandment to eat *matzah* on Passover found at Exodus 12:17) preserved in the *Mekhilta of Rabbi Ishmael* in the name of Rabbi Josiah. Playing on the fact that the Hebrew, a bit cryptically, says merely: "You shall keep the *matzot*" and also on the fact that the word for *matzot* is written with the same letters as the word *mitzvot* ("commandments"), the ancient rabbi observed that the lesson Scripture wishes to impart is two-fold: not only are the Israelites to eat *matzah* during Passover, but, just as you must not allow unleavened dough to lie around for more than a few minutes before being baked lest it rise even slightly, so must you not permit a commandment to remain unfulfilled even briefly once the obligation to perform it has devolved upon you. Instead, every opportunity life affords to worship God must be seized with eagerness and alacrity because enthusiasm enhances worship, as was clearly known to the psalmist who, addressing God, wrote, "I move quickly and without hesitation to keep Your commandments" (Psalm 119:60).

Rabbi Judah ben Tema made this point even more clearly by calling on the faithful to be "as bold as leopards, as swift as eagles, as nimble as deer, and as brave as lions" when approaching the enterprise of worship (M. Avot 5:22). By this, he meant to say that, somewhat paradoxically, submission to the will of God should not be undertaken submissively at all, but rather with zeal and eagerness, boldly and in a forthright manner, with alacrity and without hesitation.

LIFE UP YOUR HANDS IN HOLINESS

It isn't a race. It isn't a contest. You don't get to ignore some rules as a kind of reward for having obeyed others. There aren't any times out. And you don't win *or* lose, except in the sense that willing submission to the will of God can provide the context for movement forward toward attaining the great goal of living out the days of your life in the shadow of God's protective presence. For all these reasons, the journey to God along the path of submission to divine law can never be attained through disobedience to a different law, or to a different set of laws, than the one an individual is attempting to obey at any given moment. Indeed, people who transgress one of the commandments of the Torah while attempting to uphold a different one accomplish nothing of too lasting value and are akin to those ancients whom the prophet Haggai described as putting coins in a purse with holes at the bottom: the coins retain their value . . . but only theoretically and not in any practical way for the person who has lost them (1:6). Later, the sages would go even further, ruling that ownership itself is extinguished once someone no longer has any reasonable hope of recovering what one has lost. When applied to the life of the spirit, this is not at all a lesson to pass by too quickly.

In ancient times, Rabbi Eliezer expressed this truth with reference to the verse in the tenth psalm that speaks of one who "insults God by breaking bread and pronouncing a blessing" (Psalm 10:3), explaining it to reference the kind of person who, after stealing a bushel of wheat, grinding it into flour, and baking it into bread, *then* piously pinches off a corner of the loaf as the requisite baker's offering mentioned at Numbers 15:20. "Such a man," Rabbi Eliezer declared, "has insulted, not blessed, God" (B. Sanhedrin 6b). And so emerges (from, of all places, some pinched-off crumbs of bread made out of purloined flour) a great principle of spiritual integrity: it is not possible to serve and not to serve God at the same time.

The biblical qualifier for the kind of perverse worship that leads to someone feeling justified in breaking one law to uphold another is "strange," as in the references at Leviticus 10:1 and Numbers 3:4 to Nadab and Abihu as having offered "strange fire" before God. Indeed, when Scripture forbids the offering up of "strange incense" at Exodus 30:9, the point is not to rule out the use of low-grade scent as an accouterment of worship, but rather to say that God will take no pleasure in incense burnt by people who approach God's holy altar with the arrogance that comes directly from the assumption that God can be bargained with, that good deeds possess the magic power to cancel out bad ones. In the same vein, when the prophet chastises the priests of his day for bringing "repulsive bread" before God (Malachi 1:7), the reference is not to moldy loaves but to bread brought as a Temple offering by people of impure hearts and perverse motives . . . or by would-be worshipers unable—or even unwilling—to divest themselves of sin before daring to undertake the service of God, thereby ignoring the psalmist's injunction to "lift up our hands in holiness and *then* bless God" (Psalm 134:2).

In the end, the physics of the world provides the clearest model for this principle. You can walk forward or backward on a path, and you can do so slowly or quickly. You can also choose to remain immobile, thus making a conscious decision to move neither forward nor backward. But no one, not even the most agile athlete, can move forward *and* backward on the same path at the same time. Not in a world governed by the physics of three-dimensional reality. And not in the world of heartfelt spiritual enterprise either. (It's the same world.)

RATIONAL IRRATIONALITY

Raising the whole concept of seeking God through obedience to law often provokes the comment that it would be so much *simpler* if the laws presented in the Torah were rational, easy-to-understand statutes, the reasonableness of which no normal person would ever think to challenge.

That argument may sound logical at first, but founders on the fact that the laws of Scripture are best conceptualized as empty vessels that an individual so inclined may fill with spiritual yearning in an effort to transform them into actual paving stones on the path toward God, not edicts in a civil law code that need to be justified to the populace on the basis of their reasonableness and usefulness. Obedience to the so-called irrational commandments, therefore, is not irrational at all because *any* of the commandments can be successfully suffused with the kind of longing sufficiently intense to turn it into a vehicle of worship and communion. Therefore, any who decide not to obey a specific biblical law—or, even more peculiarly, who make a kind of a virtue out of the decision not to obey it—because they find its ideational substructure obscure can reasonably be said to have chosen to step away from the purposeful pursuit of their own spiritual goals by declining an opportunity to submit to the will of God.

HAPPINESS

Joy exists at the triple confluence of physical action, emotional desire, and intellectual satisfaction. As a result, true inner happiness can only come in this world to those whose activities in the physical world match their inner lives so utterly and so absolutely that they *feel* as though there is not any conflict whatsoever between, on the one hand, their desires, drives, values, and beliefs and, on the other, the circumstances of their lives as they are actually being lived. In the language of Scripture, such people are characterized as being possessed of tranquility because they exist without having to endure the war most people feel between their formally held opinions and their inmost urges and desires. In the annals of biblical heroes, this, even more than his astounding wisdom, was the greatness of King Solomon. And so was it told to David even before Solomon's birth that "a son will be born to you and he shall grow up to be a man of tranquility" (1 Chronicles 22:9).

This tranquility is the specific definition of the peace promised to them who love the commandments, as it is written "There will be great peace for those who love Your *torah* (Psalm 119:165.)" Indeed, when another psalmist wrote in his poem that the commandments of God are capable of "granting joy to the heart (Psalm 19:9)," the meaning is not that the commandments will bring the individual who performs them joy because they must, but rather that obedience to the commandments of God has the uncanny ability to bring people's outer lives into harmony with the innermost promptings of their hearts and *that*, the ancient poet is saying, is the very definition of happiness. It is also the definition of the ultimate kind of tranquility an individual may know and this is what the Talmud means to say when it teaches us that no one can ever "come into the presence of God in sadness, sloth, levity, disrespect, too-involved discourse, or too-idle chatter, but rather solely in the context of the joy afforded an individual through obedience to the commandments" (B. Shabbat 30b).

Chapter Seven

The Seventh Gate

Standing before God

If God exists outside of time and space, then how could it ever be possible for any of us meaningfully to speak—except perhaps poetically or symbolically—of standing before God? Must the answer to God's own question, "Who then can stand before Me? (Job 41:2)" not then be that no one can? And when the psalmist, describing his own spiritual yearning, wrote "My soul thirsts for God, for the living God / When shall I come and appear before God?" (Psalm 42:3), is the honest answer that he never will, just as no one ever will . . . or logically ever could? Or is it possible to speak of standing in God's presence without reference to the physics of the world? (Saying yes, however, requires explaining how that could ever be possible . . . and then demonstrating the truth of that assertion by actually proposing an actual plan for doing so.)

As readers to this point will already have guessed, I actually do think that it's possible to speak seriously and realistically about ordinary human beings being able to stand before God even without being possessed of some preternatural ability to step outside the time-space continuum. Indeed, the possibility of standing before God only truly becomes real when we finally find the inner strength to abandon the notion that experiencing the palpably real presence of God must logically require escaping from the world.

Standing before God means allowing yourself to perceive God's presence in the world as its fully perceptible core of moral worth. It means learning to understand the ordering principle that grants meaning to existence itself as a core of ethical presence capable of governing creation as the fully autonomous Will of the World. And it means allowing yourself to stand before God humbly and modestly, divested of all shreds of pride and arrogance, protective neither of your dignity nor your wealth, relying neither on your education or your professional status, trembling, fearful, defenseless, unwilling to assume that a lifetime of worshipful deeds will necessarily count for anything, and fully cognizant of the fact that most of the prayers you have recited over and over in the course of your years on earth were more *about* your personal needs and desires than they were even remotely *about* God. It means perceiving God, even if just for the briefest of moments, divested of the triple cloak of impenetrable symbol, inscrutable myth, and unlikely metaphor. And, finally, it also means accepting that, for all it is *almost* impossible to attain, the experience of standing before God is the first step anyone can take toward holiness and that taking this step itself is the fulfillment of the famous biblical injunction, "You shall be holy, for I, the Eternal, your God, am holy" (Leviticus 19:2), with the word "shall" here pointing gently to the fact that the road to Jerusalem is, at least for most of us, its own destination, that the journey is the thing, that becoming is its own version of being.

Inevitably, all this must be layered over the unsettling side-issue that no one who cannot think about God without hiding behind a protective barrier of language or symbol will ever be able truly to undertake, let alone actually to conclude, this journey to Jerusalem I keep mentioning, this journey with physical trajectory to spiritual fulfillment in God. This is the truth the biblical author meant to impart when telling about how, in the end, Elijah could only perceive God's presence in the context of perceptible/imperceptible silence: "And it came to pass when Elijah heard the sound of fragile silence that he covered his face with his cloak and went out of the cave and stood at its mouth . . . and it was then that he heard the voice" (1 Kings 19:12–13), the voice of God, speaking to him alone—which is to say: a voice from silence, existence from nothingness, faith from the sudden realization that existence and nonexistence constantly meet and then instantly diverge in a swirling vortex of divine presence that itself exists impossibly in a world that cannot possibly contain even the least significant aspect of divine reality at the same time that perceiving it—for the briefest of moments—means, by definition, taking a first step toward standing before God. It's natural to find these ideas confusing, by the way. I've devoted my entire adult life to attempting to understand them and it's taken me more than forty years to formulate them even *this* clearly.

SEEKING OUT/STANDING IN

Although Scripture teaches that God exists outside the context of space and location (and must therefore be imagined to exist neither nowhere *nor* everywhere), it is somehow possible nonetheless to turn away from God. For example, it has been the custom of Jews from time immemorial to face

Jerusalem during prayer and this has meant facing east for Jews living west of Israel. Yet the one passage in the Bible that actually describes people facing east during prayer does so only to damn them, as the prophet Ezekiel wrote: "and God took me to the Temple's inner courtyard and there, between the building [i.e., the structure that housed the Holy of Holies and its outer lobby] and the altar, I could see about twenty-five men, each with his back to [that building] and his face toward the east . . . and they were all prostrating themselves eastwards toward the sun" (Ezekiel 8:16). Who these people praying in the ancient sunlight actually were, the prophet omits to say. To me, though, they serve collectively as the paradigm of human beings so intricately involved in the effort to remain faithful to tradition that they forget that the point of all that scrupulousness and punctiliousness is not to do this or that thing according to even the most picayune details of the law, but to seek *out*, and then to stand *in*, the presence of the living God. Embracing tradition in all its endlessly byzantine detail without noticing that your back is turned to God is the precise definition of how not to come to know God through the embrace of religious ritual.

PERMANENT OBEDIENCE

The point is not to stand before God now and then, but always and permanently. But how, precisely, *does* someone go about living permanently in the presence of God? The concept itself is one of the great challenges Scripture places before the faithful and, although it feels as though the goal of standing permanently before God should be addressed after the lesser goal of existing just momentarily in God's presence is attained, the reality is that it is actually the concept of existing permanently imbued with a palpable sense of God's ongoing presence that is the *definition* of what it means, ultimately, to stand in God's presence at all. How precisely to go about attaining that, of course, is another question entirely. But the answer may have something to do with the existence of negative commandments among the divine laws of Scripture and the special nature of those specific laws.

The negative commandments are essential in this regard because they have the peculiar characteristic of permanence: since people who take to heart any of the negative commandments are in a constant state of not doing some specific thing, they can reasonably be said to be in a state of permanent observance as they perpetually refrain from doing the specific thing that that specific commandment forbids. It is to this concept of permanent observance through non-activity that the Bible refers when it declares, "Happy is one who is in a constant state of fear" (Proverbs 28:14), thus implying almost clearly that the individual who seeks joy in God will constantly fear stumbling from the path of righteousness by succumbing to the temptation to do one or another of the things Scripture expressly forbids. Indeed, when Scripture speaks of hoping for God *permanently*, as at Hosea 12:7—or of *permanently* sensing the presence of the divine presence within the perimeters of your personal ambit, as in the famous verse from the sixteenth psalm, "I see God before me always" (Psalm 16:8)—the point is specifically that people who devote themselves to the search for God must force themselves to aspire to know God not as a philosophic principle or as a lofty, but ultimately poetic, ideal, but rather as a part of the perceptible universe no less real than any other aspect of an individual's ongoing reality. This is what it ultimately means to stand in the presence of God.

When, for further example, the poet instructs readers to "seek always the face of God" (Psalm 105:4), the implication is that those who would succeed in finding God in the world cannot expend energy on their quest merely from time to time, but must seek a way to bring a sense of permanence to their spiritual efforts. They must, therefore, labor to create the sense inside themselves that they are not occasional tourists in a land not their own, but pilgrims moving forward toward the golden gates of their private Jerusalems possessed of the conviction that they will never make any real progress merely by devoting themselves occasionally to the journey. And that is why there is such special importance to the careful observance of the negative commandments: insofar as they are fulfilled by refraining from doing some specific thing and not by any specific action or activity, the faithful who keep those commandments are keeping faith every single moment of their lives with the aspect of the covenant that best suggests the never-ending nature of the quest for spiritual fulfilment in God.

It is profoundly easier for most people to feel a surge of energy at the so-called high points of the religious year—when the *shofar* is sounded at the end of the Day of Atonement, for example—but it is probably more useful in the long run to cultivate the kind of inner certainty regarding God's presence in the world that comes when worshipers comes to think of themselves as existing in a state of permanent obedience to scores of divine commandments at the same time. The theory is simple to seize . . . but, as always, the question is not whether you can seize it, but whether you can do it.

LIKE A LOST LAMB

All people, no matter how powerfully they proclaim the reality of God's presence in the world, stand before God as lost lambs wandering aimlessly in a world that by its very nature threatens and intimidates to overwhelm them at any given moment with endless tidal waves of existential doubt and worry. This point is made explicit in Scripture at the very end of the Bible's longest chapter when the poet writes explicitly that he wanders the earth "like a lost lamb" (Psalm 119:176), thus echoing Jeremiah's description of Israel itself as a "lamb aimlessly adrift" in the world (Jeremiah 50:7). According to this specific poetic image, God is the divine Shepherd concerned solely and totally with the welfare of the sheep of Israel and this in turn is the simple meaning of the most famous of all verses from the Psalms, "I want for nothing, for God is my shepherd" (Psalm 23:1). But famous though the twenty-third psalm may be, the idea that the relationship of the individual to God is similar to the one that pertains between lamb and shepherd is not unique to that passage: the author of the eightieth psalm had the same image in mind when he wrote "O Shepherd of Israel, give ear! O God enthroned upon the cherubim who leads forth Joseph like a shepherd might a flock of sheep, appear!" (Psalm 80:2).

DWELLING IN GOD'S HOUSE FOREVER

The sheep metaphor so beloved of the ancients rings a bit peculiar to moderns, and particularly to urban types who experience sheep mostly as mutton and wool, yet can still function as a profound spiritual metaphor for those willing to take seriously the scriptural worldview that identifies piety with willingness to serve God *precisely* by behaving like well-disciplined sheep prepared to place their confidence in the shepherd, to follow the rules of the pasture and the corral to which their shepherd leads them, and, more challengingly for human beings than for sheep possessed of simple ovine brains, to accept as rational and reasonable the absolute way in which the shepherd rules over the flock. The nature of the sheep's brain is actually part of the point: even the occasional sheep possessed of sufficient insight to realize that sheep, taken as a class, lack sufficient cognitive skill to understand the point of the shepherd's many rules—even *that* sheep can still accept that the shepherd assigned to its flock is just and good, and wholly dedicated to its wellbeing.

The great goal then is to be that good sheep, the one who places its confidence in the good shepherd in a way that transcends its own intellectual limitations. Indeed, when the author of the twenty-third psalm, writing as a sheep, refers to his flock's corral as a place of justice, the point is precisely that he is willing to do so even without fully understanding the various reasons for which the shepherd wishes to confine his charges to a specific area instead of just letting them wander free across the countryside. And similarly, the poet implies, should the human sheep of the divine Shepherd do their best to transcend the almost insurmountable limitations that will necessarily inhere in any effort truly to understand the wisdom of the myriad rules that bind them to God, and instead submit to those rules "for the sake of the divine name" (Psalm 23:3) and thus, at least ideally, to make them into a framework for real spiritual growth.

It follows from all this that there will inevitably be moments in the lives of the faithful during which they will find excessive theorizing about the nature of the commandments to be detrimental to their own efforts to stand before God in humility and gratitude. Indeed, there is something to be said for individuals allowing their sense of gratitude to God to overwhelm their yearning for logic and clear meaning in the world, and to allow those feelings of deep beholdenness and thankfulness to inspire them as they move slowly forward on the great path they have chosen toward spiritual wholeness in God. People who do so, if they are possessed of faith uncrippled by the absurdist notion that nothing unexplained can ever bear real meaning, will know God as their Shepherd. They will lie down in green pastures and be driven to cool waters. Instead of loathing the world as a prison in which they have been unjustly incarcerated, they will know it instead as their corral of justice. And thus shall the sheep of the divine Shepherd come to dwell in God's house forever.

BEING HOLY

To stand on a bluff overlooking the desert, you need a bluff . . . and you need a desert. To stand on what Scripture calls the holy mountain trembling before the presence of God, you need a holy mountain and you need to know where and how to seek God's presence . . . but you also need to know how to tremble.

Fortunately, trembling will come naturally to most people who find themselves in the presence of God. The bigger challenge, therefore, is to learn how to create such sacred space in the first place. As it happens, there are many different ways to approach this task, but the simplest—and the one repeatedly ordained by Scripture—involves the effort to divide down all creation into discrete realms and then to place yourself in the realm of the sacred. This notion underlies many of the Torah's laws, but it is also the truth to which Scripture is alluding subtly when it reports that the Israelites who stood at Sinai were commanded first of all to sanctify the space in which God would shortly appear to them by creating a barrier around the base of the mountain that would serve as the boundary beyond which none could go. The point, though, is not merely that the Israelites created such a boundary between the sacred and the profane, but that they were positioned on the outside, thus specifically *not* on the side of the Holy as they waited for God at the foot of the mountain on the outer side of a barrier constructed not by God but by themselves. That detail is probably missed by most, but it is the key to the story's larger lesson: that the barriers that distance us from God are more or less always self-manufactured hurdles we ourselves have erected in our own paths. Yes, it is true that God at Sinai was not held back by the barrier the Israelites erected and was more than able to transcend it and commune directly with the people. But what of people who wish to stand in God's presence and cannot be sure that God will simply ignore the barriers they have counterproductively erected between themselves and the divine presence? That awful question, Scripture leaves unasked and unanswered. But the message of Sinai, or at least of this part of the story when read in this particular way, is not so much a story told as a challenge issued.

The simplest definition of holiness rests on the assumption that the holy thing is so wholly separate from its surroundings that it can logically be said to be totally other than—and incomparable to—any other thing in the world. Among other reasons, this is why there are so few truly holy things in the world. But there is good news to consider as well in that all who obey even the *least* overtly spiritual of these dividing-down commandments—those who honor the commandment not to move the stone that marks off the limit of a neighbor's property *or* who are careful not to sow the same field with diverse kinds of crops *or* who make a point of obeying the injunction of Scripture not to wear woven garments made of linen and wool *or* who do not plow their fields with animals of diverse species held in place beneath the same yoke *or* who do not mix meat and dairy foods in their daily diets—all such people are said to be sanctifying the world in which they live by imposing the concept of separatedness and distinction upon that world and thus making the realm of the holy created by themselves suggestive of the sacred otherness of the Creator.

A poet of Jewish antiquity referred to this notion of dividing down the world into discrete domains for the sake of creating holy space as a transformational act that makes the mundane world into the kingdom of God on earth—in Hebrew, *tikkun ha-olam b'malkhut shaddai*. At its most basic, the idea is almost simple: the pious are called to seek communion with the Holy One by establishing a holy domain in real space in which they, as individual men and women, can dwell together with God in a kingdom of two. In turn, this elusive goal of coming to live together with God in a private lovers' universe of two is called the ultimate fulfillment of the scriptural injunction to love God, as it is written in the Torah, "And you shall love the Eternal, your God," (Deuteronomy 11:1), which words are followed in Scripture by the specific way an individual might actually seek to experience the love of God: "And you shall keep God's statutes and laws and injunctions and commandments all of your days" (ibid.).

JUSTICE AND WORSHIP

A basic principle—and perhaps even *the* basic principle—of all people who conduct their religious lives with absolute spiritual integrity is the fundamental assumption that all men and women, regardless of the level of faith in God they maintain or the way they choose to express or not to express that faith, are possessed of equal spiritual worth and potential in the eyes of their Creator. This basic assumption is reflected in Scripture in many places, for example in the verse from the Book of Exodus cited above, where it is decreed "You shall have only one *torah* both for the citizen and the stranger in your midst" (Exodus 12:49) or in the prophet Malachi's famous rhetorical question, "Have we not all one divine Parent? Did not one God create us all?" (Malachi 2:10). Moreover, the notion of the absolute, unequivocal equality of every individual before God is the basis of the story of creation itself and specifically of the way in which all humanity is depicted as having one single ancestor so that, in the words of the Mishnah at M. Sanhedrin 4:5, no one can rationally claim to be of superior lineage to anybody else in our world. Not if you go back far enough!

This notion of unconditional equality of worth and stature before God is the idea that rests at the generative core of all those commandments that oblige the faithful to treat their neighbors decently and fairly, and to exert themselves strenuously and forcefully in the pursuit of justice in the world. Indeed, the most famous of all these commandments, *"Justice, justice* shall you pursue that you may live" (Deuteronomy 16:20), is phrased in just that way to suggest that it is reasonable and right for the faithful to exert themselves in the pursuit of justice as though their very lives depended upon it and not merely to content themselves with securing a just verdict when they themselves are accused of crime or wrongdoing. Indeed, the word "justice" is repeated twice in the verse to teach the same lesson: to exert yourself in the pursuit of *justice* when you yourself are the accused does not require any great moral fortitude, the Torah is teaching, but vigorously and tirelessly to seek *justice* when someone else has been accused of wrongdoing—that you must do as well, and no less spiritedly or energetically than if your own future or freedom were to be hanging in the balance.

Scripture, however, does not require solely that the faithful behave fairly toward others because doing so feels decent and right, but that they do so out as a function of their conviction that all humanity is created in the image of God. In this context, the way the law works—or is supposed to work—becomes clearer: by rooting their just behavior in the conviction that all human beings, even criminals and reprobates, bear the image of God, the faithful manage to usher themselves into the presence of the divine Magistrate *precisely* by working to guarantee that justice is always done on earth . . . and by doing so even when the accused appears to have turned his or her back on God entirely. In turn, this becomes a key principle of faith as justice becomes worship and the pursuit of fairness becomes an attempt to come closer to the very God in whose image even the most appallingly guilty party is made. The repudiation of judicial prejudice and legislated bigotry becomes the sacred task Scripture assigns to all who would know God not solely because prejudice and bigotry are repugnant, but because forsaking the pursuit of justice is the ultimate sacrilege, the ultimate dismissal of Creator God from the lives of the created.

It is therefore incumbent—and totally so—on those intent on living within the divine covenant to seek justice in the world. Moreover, such people are not solely bound to seek justice in the world, but, in so doing, also to attempt to train themselves specifically not to believe that the search for fairness in the world is a worthy endeavor *because* it is the way of decent, kind people who have no desire to relate to their neighbors unfairly, but to believe instead that the pursuit of justice in the world is worthy and right *because* it is a worshipful way for human beings to come the presence of God by imitating the ways of the Almighty. In the end, it is incumbent on all people of faith to believe that there is no real meaning in qualifying behavior as decent or indecent—or as just or unjust—except by measuring it against the divine values of decency and justice. The search for justice in the world is worship. Unwarranted prejudice against any of God's creatures is blasphemy. Attempting to stand before God without acknowledging the divine image stamped on all men and women is arrogance and folly, and it is deeply counterproductive as well.

LOVING THE LAW

People trained from childhood to expect reward and praise merely for being willing to engage in any acts of formal worship at all will need to set that specific fantasy aside in adulthood and instead come to accept that worship can be valueless and base just as easily as it can be noble and profound. Indeed, even the most pious worshipers of God need to come to terms with the fact that nothing good can ever come of approaching God through the medium of submission to God's law in the style of borrowers hoping to pay off long-standing debts to a bank or of prisoners attempting to bribe their guards to free them. Just to the contrary is how things are, actually. Attitude is far more crucial than attention to picayune detail. Humility is key. Feeling almost certain that one's efforts will lead nowhere is not only rational, but wholly so. Allowing personal wants and needs to cloud the enterprise with self-interest is to degrade worship by making it self-serving, not to enhance it by making it personal. When Scripture ticks off the various boons that will accrue to the world when God is sought by the many and not by the few, it means for those lists of blessings to be suggestive of the good that can and will come from the service of God—and not as a list of promises God can later on be blamed for not having kept.

In ancient times, this truth was expressed by Rabbi Nathan with reference to the scriptural verse at Exodus 12:34 in which it is noted that the Israelites left Egypt so suddenly that they had no choice but to take their dough from their kneading troughs before it had risen sufficiently to bake into bread and then to tie that dough up in their own spare garments so they could carry it with them on their backs. Rabbi Nathan's observation is based on an obvious question: if Scripture also notes, and just four verses later in the story, that the Israelites left Egypt with huge herds of cattle and sheep, then why didn't they have the beasts of burden carry all that dough? There must have been a ton of it, too! It's a clever question, but his answer is no less so: they so loved the commandments of God (including the commandment to take the dough with them and bake it into *matzah*), teaches Rabbi Nathan, that they refused to desist from personal involvement in *even* the most banal aspect of *even* a single one of them. And carrying the dough was merely their way—their simple, elegant and graceful way—of expressing that aspect of their desire to know God in whatever way humans may. (Rabbi Nathan's lesson is preserved in section of the *Mekhilta of Rabbi Ishmael* devoted to the explication the twelfth chapter of Exodus.)

There's a key concept hiding behind that ancient lesson. People taught as children to venerate religious rites and to consider them sacred and holy will mostly have to exert themselves fully to accept that the rituals of faith are mere gestures designed to assist human beings slightly in focusing their search for God in some specific direction (as opposed to racing off in pursuit of fuzzy spiritual goals but not actually moving forward in any meaningful or purposeful direction at all). Worship doesn't "work" that way—and it certainly does not magically allow those who embrace it to step into God's favor and then, as a result, to claim all sorts of expensive prizes as their reward for having done so. It does, however, provide individuals seeking God with a way purposefully to work at finding traces of the divine in the lives they are living and then, if they are single-minded in the pursuit of their own spiritual goals, to use those traces as bricks from which to fashion a path forward that they can then follow to Jerusalem, to God. Accepting that—and taking the various implications and ramifications of that thought seriously and then running with them—is key here: as we willingly embark on an unaccomplishable journey (because none may see God and live) to an unattainable destination (because the Temple in which God chose in ancient times "to settle the divine name" has not existed in real space for almost two millennia and has never been replaced), we need to learn to be intensely grateful for even a moment's worth of insight gained through whatever means we can muster. But hardest of all is to accept the discouraging truth that the rituals of worship, for all they can work magnificently, can also fail utterly . . . just as can any tool fail to accomplish a job for which it was designed if the person wielding it is sufficiently clumsy or inept.

For Jews on the road to Jerusalem, loving the commandments will always be the key to worship undertaken with integrity. But more crucial still will be the willingness of an individual to stand before God totally imbued with yearning for God *and* thus totally divested of any sense of being put upon by the service of the divine or burdened by its exigencies. The notion that the translation of such lofty hopes and ideals into the language of mundane reality through the actual embrace of the commandments of Scripture, and not through their mere contemplation, is the defining characteristic of Judaism. But it is also the hallmark of all honest religion, no matter what its mythic base or ritual ambience.

SORCERY AND WORSHIP

The Bible could not be clearer on the worth of ritual undertaken out of the conviction, or even out of the vague expectation, that human beings can somehow oblige the Almighty to act in a *specific* way on their behalf or on the behalf of others by doing some *specific* thing or by reciting some sort of incantation. In the language of Scripture, such worshipers are called sorcerers and magicians, but only so that the Bible may specifically deny the legitimacy and validity of behavior in both categories. At Deuteronomy 18:10–12, for example, both sorcery and magic are described as abominations in the eyes of God. But equally instructive is the verse that follows, one I have already cited in these pages: "Be guileless before God" (Deuteronomy 18:13). To me, that verse means that we are to do whatever it takes to be among those who relate to God divested of guile and possessed—and possessed totally and wholly—of spiritual integrity and humility, for only pilgrims of that ilk can hope to engage in deeds of meaningful, purposeful worship and someday possibly even to stand before God. The bottommost line is that no rite or ritual, not even prayer itself, can force God to behave in any specific way and rooting an observant lifestyle in that conviction, even if delicately left untrumpeted aloud to the world, blurs the distinction between religion and superstition in a way that no honest person of faith would ever wish to countenance.

The thought that worship ever marginally tainted with self-interest is worthless will be more than a bit shocking to most. But even earlier in Scripture, this truth is implied through a gentle juxtaposition of verses: at Genesis 17:1, Abraham is commanded to come before God divested of guile, whereupon, and in the very next verse, God announces the reward for that kind of selfless service, "And I shall establish a covenant between you and between Me" (Genesis 17:2).

BEFORE THE LAW

The righteous of the world who are willing to stand before God in guileless integrity will never lie about the commandments of the Torah, not to others and certainly not to themselves, and neither will they insist that they know with certainty things that cannot be tested scientifically or empirically and which they therefore do not actually know at all. I have made that point repeatedly, but I would like now to take it to its natural conclusion.

The first step on the road to spiritual integrity is thus understanding that the history of the commandments, like the history of the biblical text itself, cannot be known with certainty and that, as a result, the worth of the commandments must be determined solely in terms of the success they do or do not have in leading the people who embrace them to God. Therefore, all err who claim that the sole reason for observing the commandments is that they constitute the direct orders of the Almighty as transmitted by Moses to the people. This is not because anyone can say with certainty that God did *not* speak them directly to Moses and command that he transmit them first orally and then in writing to the people, however, but rather because the value and worth of the commandments is unrelated to their literary history and rests solely in their ability to elevate the human soul to its Creator and to bring about a state of ongoing, intimate communion between an earth-bound human being and God whom even the limitless heavens themselves cannot contain. To decline to engage in the worship of God because there is no way to know in advance if it will be successful is no more reasonable than declining ever to speak for fear of possibly being misunderstood. Obviously, the possibility of misapprehension always exists when a word is spoken aloud. But so does the possibility of being understood by listeners exactly correctly. And that lesson can be applied to worship as well: it can well lead nowhere, but it can also lead somewhere. And so the faithful, possessed solely of that slender thread of possibility, surrender themselves to the journey and—alone and together—move forward as best they can. That is what the world it means to be a religious person. But it is also what religious people think it means to be a person, a fully human being, a self-aware child of God.

Chapter Eight

The Eighth Gate

Living with God in the World

There would be a certain impeccable logic in encouraging people seeking to live with God to flee from the world. Undisturbed by the endless exigencies of everyday life, untroubled by the inevitable friction that comes from living with spouses and children, pulled in only one direction and free to devote every waking hour to contemplative prayer and study, such people would then be able to seek God in the full-throttled way devoted, serious people address the issues in their lives they deem truly worthy of their full attention. It sounds good—and it is certainly the case that withdrawal from the world continues to be touted in at least some non-Jewish circles as the ideal context in which to undertake the journey to God—but, with certain key exceptions which only prove the general rule, it has never been the Jewish way. Nor is it the way of Scripture.

The whole notion of seeking God by running away from society rests on the notion that society itself is a kind of concession to human weakness—a second-best context that provides a setting for economic and social activity for people who lack the strength to live solely with God. But the biblical point of view is precisely to the contrary and is that society provides the context in which God may be sought and served by people able to see the same divine image stamped on every human being, no matter how fractious or difficult, and thus also to be aware *of*, and sensitive *to*, the way the enduring presence of the Creator inheres naturally—and accessibly—in creation. Among Jews, this is a rare point of universal agreement. (And you can trust me that there aren't that many.)

That basic principle can be refined in several different ways. We learn what it means to acclaim God as our divine Parent, for example, by relating to our mothers and fathers, and by becoming the human parents of our sons and daughters. We learn what it means to find in God the ultimate source of ethical morality and justice by participating in the construction of a society that treats all its citizens fairly and equitably. We learn what it means to move forward over the course of a lifetime from knowing *of* God to knowing God by learning what it means to move from knowing another human being as a casual acquaintance to cherishing that person as a true friend, as an intimate, as a soulmate in the truest sense of the word. And, in the end and if we are truly fortunate, we learn what it means to find in faith in God the ultimate medium in which to seek spiritual integration into the universe by marrying and experiencing the integration of two individuals within the context of sensuality, affection, loyalty, trust, and physical union.

To trade in all that spiritual potential for the sake of not having to deal with the endless irritations life with people inevitably entails does not seem like a very good deal at all. And, in the end, the eighth gate—the gate of living with God in the world—will only be successfully negotiated by those possessed of the courage to find in every single relationship they maintain—and not only in the ones they maintain with spouses or parents or children, but also in their relationships with neighbors and friends, with dentists and gardeners, with parking lot attendants and telemarketers and the desk clerks in motels and the vice-principals of their children's schools—to find in every single one of those ordinary, unglamorous, occasionally grating relationships a setting in which to seek God through submission to divine law. It isn't easy. We surely all do have moments when we think that retreat to a lonely desert hermitage would be just the thing. But, in the end, society is the loom upon which we are all bidden, if we can, to weave the great prayer shawl in which all who would experience God's presence in life must wrap themselves. The natural question ("How in the world could anyone go about doing that?") can be answered easily and not easily. The world is the loom and the sacred laws and statutes that govern interpersonal relationships are the threads. (That's the easy part.) But to say clearly and precisely how you—you as the idiosyncratic, specific individual you are, not merely as a member of society or some faith group within society—how precisely *you* as a totally autonomous, self-directed individual might go about weaving your own *tallit*, your own shawl—that really is for no one to know, or even to guess at, other than you yourself. (That's the part so hard it takes many a lifetime to do even poorly, let alone successfully to accomplish.)

This isn't a game you win when you collect enough gum wrappers. Life isn't a game at all, actually. The old *midrash* that teaches that God wrapped on a great *tallit* of light just before getting down to the creation of the world is meant to inspire, not merely to inform: to create a world in which the search for God has meaning and some chance of success, would-be pilgrims must wear a garment of their own weaving, one that incorporates in its warp and woof all that they are and ever could be. The loom, as noted, is the world. The skeins of thread, the sacred words of Scripture. But how exactly to weave on such a loom is something we must all learn on our own. Here's a hint, though: to learn to weave, it only makes sense to seek a weaver's counsel.

LONELINESS

The world is basically a hostile place to people of faith. Perhaps that is as it must be—or perhaps not—but, regardless, nothing is more normal than for the faithful to live in a state of mild alienation from the world in which they live and function on a day-to-day basis, and especially from scoffers who mock their yearning for God.

Being in the world and of the world, but not entirely comfortable in either capacity, is a sign of spiritual integrity. The notion, therefore, that the spiritually adept are invariably at peace with themselves and their environment is neither true nor even especially likely. And, indeed, purposefully to seek God in the world almost *requires* stepping back from the comfortable certainties that function in most people's lives as sources of comfort. On the other hand, edginess, a sense of ill ease in your own skin, an ongoing sensation of mild alienation from your own place and your personal space—those are signs that you are learning truths that people snoozing restfully at night and wandering calmly and smugly through the days of their lives won't ever even begin to acknowledge, let alone actually learn to embrace.

Community itself is a neutral concept. Indeed, life with people can be a positive, useful context for spiritual growth as long as the existence of a community of like-minded seekers lends an individual support, succor, and encouragement to continue on his or her personal path to redemptive spiritual fulfillment. On the other hand, when the presence of others serves simply to vitiate the friction and tension that could otherwise have served as energy sources capable of animating a sense of longing for God, then the presence of those others has to be evaluated negatively. This truth was no unknown to the ancients and is the precise truth to which the author of the sixty-ninth psalm meant to allude by writing "I am poor and in pain" (Psalm 69:30), and then following up that grim admission with the hopeful declaration, "But salvation in You, O God—therein shall I be exalted." Both loneliness *and* the deep encouragement that come from affiliation with a community of like-minded seekers can create the context for communion with God. Feeling obliged to choose one over the other, therefore, makes no sense at all. And, indeed, one of the great paradoxes of religion is that, for all the path to God is a journey each individual must take fully and totally alone, it is nonetheless possible to find both support and strength in the company of a whole community of *other* solitary travelers. There is only one earthly Jerusalem. But there are an infinite number of paths that lead up to its golden walls. And that infinite number of paths can accommodate an infinite number of travelers, all of them traveling alone *and* in each other's company to the city one prophet called Joy (Isaiah 22:2 and 32:13, Zephaniah 2:15) and another, Justice (Jeremiah 33:16).

THE LONG NAME

Any who insist that it is impossible for mortal beings to stand before God in the context of joyous service untainted by spoken or unspoken assumptions about the inevitability of reward demote their own worshipful acts to the pathetic level of empty slogans and self-serving rules.

In the language of Scripture, denying the possibility that the commandments of Scripture can serve as paving stones toward a life in God is called taking God's name in vain and is formally interdicted by the third of the Ten Commandments: "Thou shalt not take the name of the Eternal, your God, in vain" (Exodus 20:7 and Deuteronomy 5:11). Indeed, all who say that the commandments of the Torah cannot avail the human being seeking to live a life in God are denying the possibility that the world itself was created to serve as a kind of sacred bridge between the individual and the kingdom of heaven. And, in the end, what more abject abasement of religion than that could there be?

There is a name of God that is widely known in the world, as the Bible records: "Seth too had a son whose name was Enosh and it was in his days that the practice of crying out in the name of God was begun" (Genesis 4:26). But there are other names of God as well and among these other names is the Torah itself. (This idea, which appears several times in the Zohar, is probably best known from its exposition in the introduction Ramban—that is, Rabbi Moshe ben Naḥman [1194–c.1270], called Naḥmanides—wrote to his commentary on the Torah.) As a result, all who show respect for the commandments of God as set forth in Scripture honor the name of God and make it one with the God it designates. In the language of *kabbalah*, this is called *tikkun*. In the language of history, this is called redemption. In the context of the individual seeking a gateway to pass through on the way from banality to sublimity, from earth to heaven, from the mere intimation of divine existence to faith . . . it is called worship.

THE GATEWAY TO A LIFE IN GOD

In the same way a would-be petitioner might seek to gain access to a king's palace *first* by getting on the good side of the king's servants, so may all people seek to take some first steps toward communion with God by behaving with honor and decency toward their fellow creatures. It is for this specific reason, in fact, that Scripture summons the faithful to seek spiritual perfection *first* by mending the fabric of existence through the pursuit of justice for all and peace on earth, and only then by turning their eyes toward heaven and seeking to transcend the world by obeying those commandments that relate solely to the relationship between that individual and God. So important is this concept, in fact, that the quest for justice and peace is not described by Scripture solely as a feature of a life well lived, but as its ultimate defining feature. Indeed, the author of the thirty-fourth psalm suggests to his readers who yearn for "life" that they seek peace and pursue it (Psalm 34:15), just as the Torah commands its readers to pursue justice "so that they might live" (Deuteronomy 16:20).

In another passage, Scripture exhorts its readers not to pursue justice *per se* so that they live, however but rather to accomplish that same thing by choosing life itself (Deuteronomy 30:19). There is, however, no contradiction between the two passages because the phrase "to choose life" in the latter one refers specifically to the concept of choosing to finish the work of the Creator through personal dedication to the repair of the world, which effort certainly includes working to make the world a place of justice for all. Both verses, therefore, hint at the same truth. And, indeed, this was the truth the poet of a much later age cited above hoped to convey at the end of the Aleinu hymn that has concluded every Jewish worship service for a millennium by defining the mission of humanity as being constituted specifically of the mandate to transform the world into the just kingdom of a just God so that all humanity will understand that dedication to that specific mission is the ultimate prerequisite for worship.

This is among the most basic principles of Judaism and it could even be argued fairly cogently that it is its *most* basic principle. Therefore, consciously choosing to endure a world of prejudice and injustice because you are too busy worrying about your own ritual life is blasphemy rather than folly. (For men and women seeking God in the world, that could never be a rational choice.) Nor is it at all consonant with the spirit of Judaism to claim that the belief that the world needs repair somehow implies imperfection to its Creator. Indeed, in the Jewish conception it is precisely the opportunity to finish that which was left undone at the time of creation that constitutes one of the more accessible gateways to a life in God.

Any who insist that the world is so decrepit and so broken that it will never be repaired—or, even more bizarrely, that it *could* never be repaired—are guilty of denying the reality of God's presence in the world and perversely of suggesting that the same God Scripture describes as wholly omnipotent somehow nevertheless lacks the power to grant to men and women the possibility of seeking holiness in their lives by working to create a just world.

Not only does such an argument not make any real sense, but, at least in the Jewish conception of things, there is no more precise definition of blasphemy than proffering a theory about the world or its Maker that denies the omnipotence of God. This is not to say that many have not put forward theological theories, particularly in recent years, promoting the view that the only way for moderns to maintain serious faith in God is specifically to abandon the notion of an all-powerful God. This approach to theological thinking, however, will appeal primarily to people who focus on theological problems and see in them riddles in need of solutions instead of sources of intellectual tension and emotional stress capable of producing the kind of spiritual energy capable of propelling wholly honest individuals forward on their journeys to God.

SACRED SPACE

To live a life in God, it is necessary first of all to create a space worthy of such sacred endeavor. And, indeed, it is for this very reason that Scripture presents the idea that the world, despite the almost unbearable vulgarity that characterizes human society at its least appealing, may nonetheless be transformed into a place of sanctity and holy endeavor through the various instructions Scripture offers regarding the right way to divide the world down into discrete domains and then exerting oneself maximally to keep them separate and apart. I have referenced these laws already several times, but now I would like to address their most vexing feature, their apparent arbitrariness.

It would, for example, be hard logically or rationally to justify the law recorded at Deuteronomy 22:11 that forbids the wearing of garments made of linen and wool woven together. But what makes this seemingly arbitrary rule into a sacred task has nothing to do with training yourself to see something depraved or repugnant in a shirt made of blended linen and wool, but with the fact that people seeking to establish God's kingdom on earth are called upon by Scripture to hone their skills by surveying the space in which they live and work, and then by seeking to divide that space down into discrete domains as a way of training themselves to seek always to live in the domain of virtue and uprightness. Linen and wool are arbitrary example of how this works. Cooking meat and milk in the same pot (Exodus 23:19 and 34:26, cf. Deuteronomy 14:21) or yoking an ass and an ox to the same plow (Deuteronomy 22:10) are others. Pianists practice their scales not because anyone would describe scales as works of art, let alone as exquisite ones, but simply to train themselves the better to play works that truly are possessed of great beauty and that therefore actually do have the power deeply to move people listening to them. And the same is true of the great effort to make of the world a place of holiness: the dividing-down techniques ordained by Scripture are not their own point but merely suggestive of the great goal of coming to stand before God by creating sacred space and then, if you can find the nerve *and* the strength *and* the courage, to enter it and there to live.

With the words, "I am a stranger in the land / hide Your commandments not from me" (Psalm 119:19), the poet was saying that the threshold experience that transforms the world from a place of strangeness and lonely alienation to one of potential spiritual fulfillment is the personal decision to submit to God through obedience to the commandments, a commitment so difficult wholeheartedly to make that it is reasonable to pray to God for the strength to commit to it. Was the poet thinking specifically of those commandments that entail the effort to create in the world a domain of the sacred in which no seeker possessed of real spiritual integrity needs to feel lonely or estranged? No one can say, obviously. But it sounds cogent to me!

IN THE IMAGE OF GOD

To assert that God can be found in the fabric of human society for the simple reason that every human being is created in the image of God is one of those scriptural truths that is dramatically easier to declaim than to explain. But what *does* it mean? Surely not that human beings resemble God in the way that lambs resemble sheep! But it can also hardly mean that human beings resemble God in the way that reflections resemble the things they reflect or the way children and their parents occasionally look remarkably like each other. Instead, the idea is best understood as a kind of poeticized assertion that there is a basic, existential similarity between Creator and creation, one that, for all it can neither be explained nor described adequately in human language, can nevertheless be exploited to grant human beings the potential to feel themselves to bear some sort of personal connectedness to the way that God exists in the world. (It is, in fact, this inscrutable, inexpressible similarity that allows humanity and God to coexist in the same universe without the reality of God's presence in the world making it impossible for human beings truly to feel that they exist in it at all.)

Furthermore, many of the commandments of Scripture appear specifically designed to enable the faithful to build a kind of bridge to the divine realm out of planks fashioned of the various ramifications and implications of the notion that humanity is created in the image of God. For this reason, all who stand up in the presence of the elderly come that much closer to experiencing communion with God by virtue of having acknowledged in someone close at hand the image of God in which even the frailest among us too are created. Scripture hints at this truth in the specific way in which it commands respect for the elderly too: the commandment to "rise up before the hoary head and show respect for the elderly" (Leviticus 19:32) is followed directly by the injunction to fear God (ibid.), the point being that the faithful can demonstrate their conviction that *all* humanity is created in God's imagine by showing respect for *all*, specifically including even the least robust or vigorous.

For most of us, this is the framework in which we will best understand the commandments that govern relationships between people. Indeed, the best opportunity most of us will ever have to find God in the world rests precisely in the fact that every biblical injunction to treat others with respect and dignity has at its core the notion that, by behaving in that specific way, we also show respect for the God in whose image those human beings were and are created. And the inverse, needless to say, is also true: denying that someone is created in God's image because of the depravity of that person's behavior is tantamount to denying the potential for decency and reform that inheres in every single human being created in God's image, which category includes all human beings with no exceptions at all.

It is for this reason that ancient Jewish texts stress that we should hate the sin and the not the sinner—because, for all sins should be reviled as offenses against God, sinners themselves are human beings who bear the stamp of the Creator in and on their flesh and, as such, are by their very nature possessed of the ability to live lives of goodness and integrity. To insist otherwise is specifically *not* to see the image of God in the face of every single one of God's creatures, including both those the least inclined to think of themselves in that way and also those whose comportment in the world fails to suggest even the most marginal willingness to submit to the will of God.

LIFE AS WORSHIP

Let's stay for just a while longer with the idea that people, for all they are born of their parents, are also reasonably referenced as born of God. The scriptural references to the idea can be divided easily into two categories: those that tell the actual story of how God made Adam and Eve and those more about humankind itself than about the first couple. The verses in the former category are the more famous, but those in the second category are the more challenging. Indeed, the notion that existence from cradle to grave is a gift from God—despite our obvious human parentage—is put forward in Scripture as much to challenge as to inform. When, for example, the Levites in the days of Ezra and Nehemiah included the phrase "You grant life to all" (Nehemiah 9:6) in their prayers, the clear intention was not merely to assert that God created Adam and Eve on the first Friday, but that God continues to animate every living soul and that the existence of those individuals' earthly parents in no way nullifies that assertion. (Those specific words from Nehemiah, by the way, are recited in synagogue every single day of the year as part of the Morning Service and will be familiar to all who attend regularly. As such, they hardly constitute any sort of secret doctrine known only to true cognoscenti.)

In the end, there is no idea people seeking God's presence in their lives have to work more strenuously at accepting than this one. It is one thing, after all, to assert that God is not to be acclaimed merely as the one-time Creator of a single human being in the manner of a potter who creates a pot on his wheel only to have the integral, ongoing part of his relationship with his creation end the moment it emerges from the kiln. But to replace the potter-and-pot model with the idea that God is the land in which we all live every day of our lives and the ongoing source of our moral vitality and the wellspring of our emotional and intellectual vigor—that is the great hurdle that all must clear who would know the Creator through personal engagement with creation.

When written out baldly, it almost sounds easy. But nothing could be further from the truth than the assertion that accepting these ideas and making of them the loom on which to weave a life in God is a simple matter of will or of conviction. Seizing the place of God in the real world is a challenge every person of faith faces every single day. And, indeed, for all accepting God as the source of vitality, creativity, and intelligence in the world should be the natural condition for all who profess to be interested in living lives of spiritual integrity, the truth is that getting to that level of confident acceptance of that specific concept is a goal only theoretically attainable for most. To surrender your sense of personal autonomy on the altar of submission to the will of God is a challenge most take a lifetime successfully to negotiate, if indeed they ever do successfully negotiate it. When viewed in this light, life becomes a kind of journey from wherever it is we are when we set out to the moment at which we accept ourselves truly to be children of God to the great goal we set for ourselves which for people of faith will always be the integration of the self into the great ocean of being we call God. When Scripture transparently says, "You are children of the Eternal, your God" (Deuteronomy 14:1), it is stating a simple truth and inviting us to spend the days of our lives approaching it and, if we are able, coming slowly to accept it and its implications for the way we live.

AT THE BOUNDARY OF MUNDANE AND HOLY

When God is called the Holy One or the source of holiness in the world, it implies that God is wholly other both from the world and from the men and women in it, and also that God exists in a unique context of being that cannot bear honest comparison to any other kind of reality. This domain of divine reality was called "heaven" by some ancient authors, but the ancient prophet

Habakkuk called it "the holy palace" and called on humanity to acknowledge as much with the famous words, "the Eternal is in God's holy palace / be ye still, all people on earth" (Habakkuk 2:20). By calling on the faithful to be still, he meant to warn them against pressing the metaphor of divine existence too forcefully. God does exist, the prophet was saying, but only if we deny the word "exist" any meaning derived from the contemplation of human existence. And the prophet's solution to his own problem is still the best: believe in God's existence, he recommends, but say nothing of it at all lest you end up speaking nonsense.

Few and very far between are the people in the world who take that advice to heart. Still, it is a profound principle of faith that individual men and women somehow nevertheless do possess the ability to locate the boundary between the mundane and the holy, and then, having done so, to place themselves wholly within the sphere of the divine through the sheer force of their moral will to do so. This experience is also called by different names: living in God, nestling beneath the wings of the Shekhinah, visiting in the divine palace, and many others. Indeed, this is the underlying point of the verse from the twenty-seventh psalm that reads, "One thing do I ask of God / for that single thing do I yearn / that I should dwell in the house of God all the days of my life, that I should gaze on the beauty of God, and that I should visit in the divine palace" (Psalm 27:4). Surely, the reader immediately asks, dwelling in God's house, gazing on God's beauty, and visiting in the divine palace are three things, not one! But the poet wishes to teach his readers something profound and useful with his only apparently poor arithmetic: that visiting in the domain of the holy and the sacred, establishing some kind of sensory communion with the reality of the divine, and living a life in God are all poetic restatements of the same underlying possibility that beckons the faithful forward in all places and at all times.

GRATITUDE AND SUBSERVIENCE

Maybe we should begin again. Living with God in the world means using the rituals of worship to develop a sense of your place in the world and the degree to which that place has become an arena for true spiritual growth. A good example of how this works derives from the special set of commandments based on the notion that God may be perceived as a kind of cosmic Landlord presiding over a vast world populated by tenant farmers and sharecroppers toiling to bring forth bread from fields not their own. As a result, all who conduct themselves in this world as though they were the masters of their own estates instead of training themselves to feel like laborers toiling away on someone else's property are guilty, at the very least, of insolence born of naiveté regarding their place in the world.

In ancient times, King David felt this point to be of such especial importance that he assigned the task of composing and performing hymns of thanksgiving to a special family within the tribe of Levi, the family of Asaph, as we read in the Book of Chronicles, "At that time, David assigned the primary responsibility of giving thanks to God to Asaph and his brethren" (1 Chronicles 16:7). Even this, however, did not suffice in David's mind and, eventually, he was obliged to add even more to the choir of thanksgiving: Heiman and Jeduthun and others "who were specifically designated by name to give thanks to God, Whose mercy endures forever" (1 Chronicles 16:41). Indeed, even centuries later, a special choir of thanksgiving was maintained in the Temple and it was the members of this choir, Scripture relates, that assisted Nehemiah ben Ḥakhaliah in the rededication of the walls of Jerusalem in early Second Temple times.

In our day, with neither Temple nor Temple choir, the obligation to use the rituals of faith to construct a life in God based on deeply felt gratitude to God has passed from the families of Asaph, Heiman and Jeduthun to all who seek to know God through the specific media of thanksgiving, beholdenness and gratitude. Indeed, it is precisely through the cultivation of these emotions—each rooted in the notion that God is the ultimate Owner of the terrestrial house in which all humanity dwells—that moderns seeking to live lives in and of God will find the framework for their first, tentative steps forward on the pilgrim's path they have chosen to wander.

REWARDS

Although it is true that Scripture occasionally notes the reward for the performance of a specific commandment is a long life lived "on the land God shall grant to you" (Exodus 20:12, Deuteronomy 5:16, cf. Deuteronomy 22:7), the point Scripture is making is not literally that there are several among the commandments that have the amazing ability to grant those who keep them long lives and that these commandments are therefore more valuable or more important than the rest. Indeed, the fact that the commandments so singled out by Scripture all involve kindness or respect toward parents, including the parents even of animals, provides the key to their ultimate meaning: the lesson is that those who behave decently toward their own parents—and even those who behave with compassion and goodness toward a mother hen or a cow in the company of her calves—will acquire a sense of God as their own heavenly Parent and, in so doing, will feel their lives to be blessed with profundity and meaning as they come to see themselves as children of God living out long lives in the land God has granted them, that land called Redemption in which the pious seek to dwell all the days of their lives.

Therefore, all who keep the commandments of Scripture out of some vague assumption that, in so doing, they can oblige God to bless them with some different blessing that they powerfully desire—those people are the ones specifically damned by the great Talmudic teacher Rava, whose lesson, preserved in the Talmud at B. Berakhot 17a, was that it would be better for the individual who does the commandments for any purpose other than the pure worship of God not to have been born in the first place. Rava chose a rather extreme (and more than slightly off-putting) way of expressing himself, but that doesn't make his underlying point untrue. And, indeed, the reality in our day is that it actually *is* entirely possible to be faithful to an intense regimen of ritual observance while at the same time growing ever more distant from God by allowing your worshipful deeds and words primarily to be about yourself.

A BRIDGE THAT DOES AND DOES NOT EXIST

Seeking God in the world requires embracing the great paradox that the effort to sanctify daily life means exerting yourself maximally to make the hours and minutes, even the seconds, of your life into a bridge to God that exists at least slightly within the boundaries of space and time at the same time it leads to communion with a God who exists wholly outside both of space and of time. This image of crossing a bridge to the knowledge of God has its darker side as well, however, because even the slightest amount of falsehood or the smallest breach of integrity can cause the bridge to collapse and pitch those standing on it into a chasm of self-delusion and absurdity. Was it perhaps such people that the author of the tenth psalm had in mind when he wrote about the wicked being ensnared in traps they themselves have set (Psalm 10:2)? It could have been! In our world, we would never use the language of wickedness to describe people whose worshipful acts are more about themselves than about God. Nor perhaps should we . . . but moderns would do well nonetheless to wonder what could have prompted the ancient poet to write in such a bitterly negative way about people whom we ourselves tend to admire for their religious fervor even if we can see clearly that the mindset motivating that fervor is tainted with self-interest. Are we just kinder and more tolerant than our spiritual forebears? Or are our standards just so low when it comes to religious observance that it seems almost bizarrely nitpicky to base our assessment of someone's behavior on its motivating factors at all?

This notion of worship as a kind of bridge from the world to God does not entail any sort of obligation on the part of the faithful to create artificial contexts in which to perform the commandments, however. Instead, Scripture prefers simply to require that those who wish to make their lives into personal, private bridges to God perform the commandments of Scripture in the order they devolve naturally upon them without feeling obliged to perform those commandments that do not fall to them in the context of the lives they are actually living. This does not, however, negate the dictum of the great Talmudic teacher, Resh Lakish, who taught that a Jew must never pass up the opportunity to perform a commandment (B. Yoma 33a). Indeed, both lessons fit nicely together: just as you are not obliged to create artificial contexts in which to seek God, so are you equally obligated not to pass up those opportunities to make your life into a bridge toward God when they do naturally occur in the context of real life. For example, Deuteronomy 22:8 ordains that anyone who builds a home with a flat roof must install a kind of fence around the outer part of the roof lest someone accidentally fall off and die as a result, yet nowhere does tradition suggest that the pious have some sort of obligation actually to build a house with such a roof merely to oblige themselves to erect a fence around its perimeter. Nor does Scripture suggest, even obliquely, that we are somehow obligated somewhere along the way to purchase a field so as to be able to leave its corners for the poor to harvest on their own or to leave any forgotten sheaves of grain in place for the poor to take for themselves or their families.

The core idea is that Scripture specifically does not wish for the faithful to construct artificial worlds in which to seek the God of truth, but rather to sanctify daily life in the context of the lives they are actually living. God, who is the ultimate reality, is thus to be sought in the context of the reality the faithful know and experience daily.

ALONE TOGETHER

Although the most basic—and honest—of all depictions of the journey to God is that of the individual divested of pride and arrogance slowly approaching God throughout the days and years of a lifetime spent on the solitary path to personal redemption, there is also great benefit in seeking God as part of a community and thus did the psalmist write, "I am the friend of all who fear You and who keep Your laws" (Psalm 119:63).

In other psalms, the paradox is put more bluntly. The author, for example, of the twenty-sixth psalm writes "I walk forward in my own guileless company" (Psalm 26:11), only to follow that comment by saying "In great crowds, do I bless God" (Psalm 26:12)—which is to say, although it is so that the road to faith in God is by its very nature one an individual must wander alone, it is still possible to enjoy the company along the way of other lonely wanderers who themselves are moving forward, alone and together, toward the great goal of communion with the living God.

The key to real spiritual growth is learning to embrace this paradox without becoming upended by the impossibility of living alone *and* together, of seeking solace in solitude *and* in a great congregation of worshipers, of walking toward Jerusalem as a solitary pilgrim on a wholly personal street *and* of approaching the Holy City as part of a huge throng of like-minded supplicants. This is the great paradox around which religious life revolves and, as such, it by definition cannot be resolved. (It wouldn't be a paradox if it could be.) But neither does it have to be denied. Instead, it can be embraced, the very un-unravelability of its interdependent yet mutually exclusive truths providing the kind of tension capable of moving pilgrims forward on the road that leads toward the knowledge of the unknowable God.

A life in God is its own reward, clearly. But coming to terms with the fact that the quest for such a life—and its attainment—can only be contemplated in the context of insoluble riddle and impenetrable paradox is crucial for all who would undertake a journey to somewhere and nowhere, to a God whom human beings may know to exist yet who cannot exist in any way human beings can fathom, who both *is* and *is not* in a swirling, disorienting vortex of reality and unreality granted fathomability only by the sheer force of the human will to live a life in God unhampered by reason, logic, or rationality. Lying about God is blasphemy. But embracing the paradoxes that any effort to know God, or even meaningfully to know *of* God will naturally engender, is not sinful behavior at all. Just to the contrary, there is a certain nobility that inheres in the quixotic enterprise of seeking to know the unknowable God through the medium of ritual and rite . . . as long as the process does not lead would-be pilgrims to abandon their intellectual or spiritual integrity by lying to themselves about what they are doing. The road to Jerusalem can never be paved with fantasies or half-truths. Or perhaps it can be—but not by anyone actually interested in getting there.

Chapter Nine

The Ninth Gate

Loving God

In the end, it all comes down to love. Love is the context in which we all grow, in which we slowly become aware of the contents of the inmost chambers of our own hearts by opening them to the love of other people. Love is thus the context in which human beings step outside themselves to pierce into other people's personal universes not merely because they can or because they wish to, but because they have finally come to understand that the road to self-knowledge leads—paradoxically but unavoidably—through the knowing of others. This is not as simple as it sounds, however: the discrete sphere of being that each of us inhabits can only be penetrated by another when that other individual is forcefully enough driven forward by desire to lose track of what can and cannot logically be, thus becoming able to bypass the physics of the natural world and create a doorway into a previously nonexistent realm that now—also paradoxically—exists unencumbered by rules of any sort at all at the confluence of ecstasy and introspection, the very intersection at which Scripture teaches that the door to divine communion too may successfully be found. In other words, only by learning to know another can we learn to know ourselves. And only by coming to know ourselves can we come to know, or even come to know of, the great Other that is the God of the world and its Creator. It is, therefore, only by experiencing the overpowering desire to love another that we can even begin to seize the implications—and they are beyond counting—of the commandment that exists at the liturgical core of all worship: "Love the Eternal, your God, with all your heart, with all your soul and with all the intensity of which you are capable" (Deuteronomy 6:5).

Chapter 9
TRUE LOVE

Like the love of lovers, the love the faithful feel for God is—or should be—selfless and pure, and totally untainted by base expectations about what they may rationally expect back from God in return for years of obedient service. In biblical terms, this is the spiritual equivalent of the love of David and Jonathan that was characterized by the ancient rabbis as "the kind of love that, because it depends on no other thing, will never fade" (M. Avot 5:18), the kind of love that manifests itself as the longing that flows directly from the chambers of one person's heart into the chambers of another's and which is wholly independent of either party's wish for self-gratification or personal gain.

This lesson was taught in ancient times by Rabbi Eleazar, who based himself on a verse from the 112th psalm that declares happy "the individual who fears God *and* whose total desire is for the divine commandments" (Psalm 112:1). To this, Rabbi Eleazar noted that the pious, by definition, are those whose yearning for God may be characterized as love precisely *because* it manifests itself as uninhibited desire wholly unrelated to any rewards, imagined or real, that that love could someday conceivably yield.

There is also another kind of love in the world, of course: the kind that manifests itself in the sphere of religion as an endless series of worshipful acts undertaken *precisely* as a function of an individual's hope for some specific reward. In Jewish terms, this was the debased passion that Antigonos of Sokho wished obliquely to condemn when he noted, as cited above, that, *if* they wish their efforts to bear fruit and to move them closer to personal salvation in God, *then* those who obey the laws of the Torah must do so not in the manner of servants who serve their masters and mistresses for the sake of some anticipated reward, but rather in the manner of faithful, dedicated servants who serve out of a deep sense of commitment to the concept of service itself . . . and out of the pure and selfless desire that their masters' will be done. (Antigonos' lesson is preserved in the Mishnah at M. Avot 1:3.)

To underscore how important it is that the love for God never be tainted with ulterior motive, Scripture refers in the most extreme terms to people whose service to God is based wholly or even mostly on the benefits they expect to accrue to themselves as a result of their fidelity. The author of the 119th psalm, for example, had such people in mind when referring harshly to the "cursed arrogant who err in the performance of Your commandments" (Psalm 119:21). But many other passages in Scripture speak equally disparagingly about those who attempt to use the commandments of Scripture for personal gain.

From a spiritual point of view, there is no greater error than forgetting that all who undertake the service of God out of the conviction that they will be rewarded for their efforts in some specific way they *already* have in mind are dooming their efforts from the outset. Such self-centered worshipers may be compared to the kind of people who enter stores with long lists that they intend to read aloud while the shopkeeper scurries about gathering all the various things they have come to purchase. Although it is the customers who are the guests in the shopkeeper's shop, they behave as though they are the masters and the shopkeeper, their servant. But, of course, the shopkeeper runs around seeking to earn their favor precisely because, for all the shop in question may formally and legally belong to the shopkeeper, the latter is nevertheless totally dependent on the custom of customers if it is to stay open for business. To the extent that that is so, it might be considered slightly reasonable to treat the shopkeeper as a servant . . . but to approach the service of God in the manner of an imperious customer reading out a shopping list to a servile shopkeeper is to degrade the concept of fidelity to the law as a manifestation of love to the level of a business transaction. And that point is key because degraded love artificially set in place as a means to an end has the same minuscule chance of enduring in the spiritual context as it does between earthly lovers.

LOVERS AND GUESTS

Most people who yearn for God in this world rarely, if ever, manifest that yearning specifically as the wish to be judged by the Judge of the world or micro-governed by the Sovereign of the universe. Instead, their desire is rooted in their hope to attain a level of intimacy with God so intense that it makes it reasonable for them to think of their souls as being bound up inextricably with the great Over-Soul, with God, in a relationship of mutual succor and supportive caring. And although, as noted, the scriptural model for this kind of deeply supportive friendship is the relationship between David and Jonathan, the Bible does not limit this kind of relationship to relatives or even to earthly lovers, but rather teaches that "there are intimate friends even closer than siblings" (Proverbs 12:23). God does not function in the world solely as Sovereign and Magistrate, then, but also as caring Partner-in-Dialogue to all who pursue communion with the divine in truth and with integrity.

All who seek this kind of intimacy with God are called to divine service no less meaningfully than any others, only perhaps with greater urgency. And this too is mirrored in the Bible in many different passages. Abraham, for example, is at one juncture heard complaining that he is lonely and without progeny in the world, but the very next verse notes that his dilemma was resolved "when the word of God came to him" (Genesis 15:4)—and so will obedience to the word of God bring love and a deep and abiding sense of companionship to any who feel alienated from the world and cut off from society. Similarly, when the psalmist says of himself, "I am a stranger in the land" (Psalm 119:19), and then follows this first remark with the prayer that God "conceal not the commandments" from him, his point surely is that adherence to Torah law will bring an individual to know Friend God as the source of caring and succor in life, and not merely as the source of judgment and governance.

Especially directed toward the engenderment of such feelings in the hearts of the devout are the laws that inspire those who observe them to think of themselves as guests in God's house rather than as the kings and queens of their own tiny domains. These commandments are many—to be hospitable to strangers, to be kind to the weak and the powerless, to give charity freely and unbegrudgingly to the poor, gladly to eat the foods declared licit to eat without carping about the arbitrary natures of the dietary laws, to bless God in gladness and deeply felt satisfaction after every meal—but although they are many in terms of their detail, the same basic proposition underlies them all: that is it possible for human beings to find in God the source of warmth and friendship in the world . . . and thus to find God not only out there in the world and its parts and its people, but also—even more accessibly—in the inmost chambers of their own hearts as well.

THE HEART OF THE WORLD

The cornerstone of all worship is the obligation freely accepted to love God with the totality of the inner strength and fortitude musterable from the deepest recesses of the human heart, just as King Josiah instructed the people of Jerusalem to worship God "with all their hearts and with all their souls (2 Kings 23:3)."

Like all love worth the name, however, this love cannot be limited to the sphere of the intellect and requires physical expression in the world for it to exist in any truly satisfying way for the parties concerned. This truth, no less romantically and erotically charged than intellectually and emotionally challenging, is presented in a different chapter of Scripture, however, when the commandment to "love the Eternal, your God" is followed with specific instructions for transforming the injunction from the sphere of the theoretically possible to the domain of the actually doable: ."..and you shall keep God's standards, laws, statutes and commandments in the course of every single one of all your days" (Deuteronomy 11:1).

Is it truly possible to will love into existence? Most people would say no, that that would be an impossibility, that the human heart cannot love on command. And yet it is also so that God functions as the heart of the universe in a way so potent and so deeply enthralling that, against all odds, it somehow *is* possible for individuals possessed merely of the *desire* to love God to allow their hearts to be attracted naturally to the Heart of the World, which is God, in the natural way that intimacy presumed yet not quite yet realized can serve earthly lovers as the framework for their initial, tentative steps into each other's space *and* into each other's heart.

The love of human lovers, with all its emotional, romantic and erotic baggage, is thus the great model life provides for those seeking to love God with all their hearts. But, for all human love can serve as an effective training ground for those who would love God, it is also essential to recall that the model is imperfect and that the love of God, for all it *resembles* the love of lovers, is also something totally unique and different.

THE HOLY CITY

There is a specific set of commandments within the larger body of scriptural law that possess the special capacity to bring those who observe them closer to the love of God. In this context, love is defined as the acquisition of perfect and absolute faith in God as the sacred center of existence and as the quintessence of equilibrium and symmetry in the world, just as the love that may exist between two earthly lovers is defined as the acquisition of absolute confidence on the part of the one that the other is the center of his or her world and the very heart of the reality in which he or she lives.

For this reason, there is special importance to those commandments that have at their core the concept of the sublime holiness of Jerusalem, for it was in Jerusalem that the ancients located the Foundation Stone they imagined to be the point at which the creation of the world began, just as in the ancient lesson preserved in Leviticus Rabbah 20:4 in the name of Rabbi Yosei ben Ḥalafta, who, when asked how the Foundation Stone got its name, answered that it is called the Foundation Stone because it was in that place that the universe was founded.

All who serve God through the commandments that add to the sanctity of Jerusalem, which is the heart of the earth, approach God, who is the Heart of the World. Therefore, all who would obey the commandment to love God should exert themselves especially to observe those commandments specifically linked to the sanctity of Jerusalem, the Holy City that exists unfettered by spatial or temporal coordinates at the center of existence. The commandment to make three annual pilgrimages to Jerusalem is phrased in the Torah in a way that makes this point obvious. Surely, you might object, people called to believe that God exists in all places and inheres in all things hardly need to visit the Temple of God because it is there alone that "the face of God may be seen" (cf. Exodus 23:17 and 4:23 or Deuteronomy 16:16). There may well be some logic to that argument, but the deeper point of the commandment to come three times annually to Jerusalem as a pilgrim is to suggest that all who would seek to know God as the center of being and the heart of existence must travel to Jerusalem, the Holy City, and attempt to add to its sanctity through the sheer force of their will to acknowledge God in that place as the source of holiness in the world.

LOVING GOD

The basic principle that underlies all biblical law is that the right—or at least the permission—to approach God, the source of holiness in the world, is embedded in the ability to self-sanctify by obeying the commandments of Scripture and thus to become worthy of such an encounter. Indeed, this notion—that the commandments make sacred the world—itself functions as a kind of ideational bridge between those below who yearn for holiness and God, who is the source of holiness on high.

In turn, this elaborate endeavor to sanctify life and to recognize God as the source of holiness at the center of creation *also* makes those who seek holiness and who sanctify the world with their acts of fealty and worship into partners of God in the redemption of the world. And this two-sided effort shared by the faithful below who yearn to know God as the source of holiness in the world and God on high, whom the Torah and the prophets depict both as the source of holiness and the agent of sanctification in that same world, this *shared* endeavor is how Scripture defines the love of God that the faithful are commanded to seek and, if they are able, to attain. God is not love. (What would that even mean?) But love is nonetheless the great and fully accessible medium in which God may be experienced by individuals able to open their hearts unrestrainedly to the desire *for* God as it morphs slowly but surely over the years first into the knowledge *of* God and then to an ongoing sense of God's presence not in the sky and not in the world but in the individual heart of each individual pilgrim as the walls of the Holy City suddenly glimmer visibly in the distance and the possibility of actually arriving there transcends the theoretical and, in the twinkling of an eye, becomes fully real.

Chapter Ten

The Tenth Gate

Cleaving unto God

God can be called many things—the world beyond the world, the core and perimeter of existence, the heart and soul of being, the quintessence of love, the moral center of the universe, the great and never-ending source of law, the effulgent unity of opposites, the One, the Name . . . to say only the ones that come the most readily to mind—but for those goodhearted seekers of all faiths who yearn for God with purity of heart and intensity of spirit, it will almost surely be as the fulcrum of insoluble paradox and un-unravelable riddle that the Almighty will be the most familiar. Acting as the possibility of impossibility in a world that both does and also absolutely cannot contain even the *least* consequential aspect of divine reality, God presents the faithful—or, rather, the would-be faithful—with the prospect of finding a way to the deepest level of existence by undertaking a journey that *may* not exist to a goal that *does* not exist along a trajectory that *cannot* exist to a level of faith that can only be embraced by accepting—and by accepting wholeheartedly and without reservation—the great secret of human being which is that arcane ambiguity that the *Zohar* calls the *raza d'mehemnuta*, the mystery of faith: that although God may not be known, the knowledge of God somehow remains possible.

This great goal is called cleaving unto God, but, like all terms conceived within the framework of purely symbolic language, it merely points *at*, without actually referring *to* (let alone delineating clearly) that which it is supposed to denote. But because all roads to God lead through this crux of meaning and the impossibility of meaning, any who realistically seek to cleave unto God must do so along the landscape of symbolism and myth. Because, for example, God is the heart of existence, faith may be sought within the chambers of the human heart . . . and through the promulgation of kindness and the pursuit of love. Because God is the moral ground of being, faith may be sought through the informed contemplation of the world . . . and through the establishment of an ethical society devoted to divine values. Because God is the mind of the of the universe, faith may be sought within the labyrinthine matrices of the human brain . . . and through the informed manipulation of the intellect through textual study, meditative exercise, and mindful, contemplative prayer.

All of these avenues are real paths that any human being can take toward faith despite the fact that none of them actually exists or ever could exist. The journey out *is* the journey in. Searching *is* finding. Despair *is* hope. Impossibility *is* possibility. Embracing paradox *is* the resolution of paradox. Is *is* is not. And so, the great goal of cleaving unto God—of embracing faith *in* God and the love *of* God without becoming crippled by delusion and self-serving fantasy—that elusive objective is both possible and impossible, the latter because it must be and the former because it somehow is.

ONE RULE IN LOVE

Any who claim to believe that there is only one God must logically *also* feel bound not to believe that the ability to cleave unto God inheres in one specific kind of human being more potently or really than in any other.

It is therefore a renunciation of traditional faith to behave as though the one God did not create all humankind or as though all living souls do not have one heavenly Parent. (The prophet's rhetorical questions preserved at Malachi 2:10 and cited above, "Have we not all one divine Parent? Did not one God create us all?" speak directly to that point.) Therefore, all who deny that there is one God for all humanity—and that, therefore, all the world's people are equally capable of coming to love God and to serve God in awe and trembling, and to cleave unto God with all their souls and with all their hearts—such people may feel justified in their beliefs but what they are really doing is turning away from the image of God imprinted on the faces of all the world's people and thus also from God who created humankind with that specific feature. (Surely all who worship the *one* God must necessarily be worshiping the *same* deity!) And this too: if there can be rules in love, then there can be rules in worship. But love inhibited is hardly love . . . and the same applies to the love of God. It feels as though those thoughts cannot both be true. And yet not only *are* they both true, but it is precisely from the tension between them that derives, or that *can* derive, the energy to propel us forward both on our personal journeys to the love of another soul and also on our private/public journeys to the love of God.

MALE AND FEMALE

The possibility of cleaving unto God in a relationship of lifelong intimacy is precisely the same for men and women and this is the meaning of the verse, "God fashioned humankind in the divine image, creating on the same day both men and women" (Genesis 5:1–2)—that is to say: the physical differences between women and men are incidental to the spiritual equality described in the language of Scripture with reference to their common creation in the image of God. Therefore, any who insist that the ability of women to submit to the will of God, successfully to immerse themselves in meditative study, and to worship through the traditional media is less real than the analogous set of abilities and possibilities among men—such people are guilty of denying the fact that the common origin of men and women in God points almost inarguably to a common destiny as well. And yet women were for millennia excluded from full participation in Jewish life, both communal and ritual, and the same is true for other faith groups as well.

For Jews, however, the key point has to be that denying women the right to fulfill any of the commandments of the Torah is inconsonant, and fully so, with the basic principle that both women and men are equally called to the worship of God, which point in turn is the deeper meaning behind the verse "In joy and gladness shall they be brought into the palace of the king / to that place shall they surely go" (Psalm 45:16), a verse that can grammatically only be referencing women. (This is clear in the original but not in translation—yet another reason to learn Hebrew!)

THE JOURNEY

For many people, it is helpful to conceptualize the lifelong search for communion with the divine as a kind of journey toward God. And indeed, other than physical reality, growth toward God has so many of the trappings of a journey undertaken from one place to another that thinking of the spiritual life in that specific way makes sense provided you are able to bear several fundamental truths in mind every step of the way. Of these, the most important is that the journey has neither trajectory nor itinerary, neither beginning nor end. Therefore, travelers do not actually move from one place to another in the course of their travels. Nor does the destination exist at all in any but the most extended sense of the word possible.

Because it leads to a destination that exists wholly outside human experience, the journey to God cannot be described other than poetically or symbolically in any human language. Therefore, people who sell guidebooks to others seeking to undertake this journey without mentioning that their books are works of poetry, myth, fable, metaphor, and symbol are, by definition, attempting to convince people that they can describe that which is by definition indescribable and as such far beyond the reach of even the most articulate human speaker. It is, of course, possible to move forward toward a life in God, but only on the condition that would-be travelers constantly recall that the intellectual concept of God as a physically existent destination attainable by undertaking an arduous journey from one place to some other place is seriously misleading and cannot be taken as reflective of anything even remotely like literal truth. In turn, this is the meaning of Rabbi Ami's adage cited above to the effect that God is the Place of the World, even though the world is not the place of God (Bereshit Rabbah 68:9).

SELF-IMPOSED ROADBLOCKS

The journey to God may be undertaken successfully only by someone so utterly and deeply possessed of absolute intellectual integrity and spiritual honesty that even the slightest hint of self-deception becomes an impassable roadblock that makes it impossible for that individual to continue on at all. Therefore, all who would step outside of the physics of the world to seek God must first accept—and accept absolutely and totally—that even casual lies about God have the power to ruin even the most assiduous devotion to the performance of ritual and rite, and thus almost inevitably to distance those who tell them from the very God whom they wish so ardently to approach.

HONESTY AND LONGING

The religious life is an old *sukkah*, an old hut that has undergone so many different repairs over the millennia that the original building has actually vanished entirely. That there originally *was* a building—the original structure to which all the repairs were done—seems impossible to doubt. And that God was the Maker of this original structure is a basic principle of faith. The possibility of finding God in the world will therefore be directly related to someone's ability to live in this tottering hut and through the building to seek the Builder without becoming all tangled up in the interesting but ultimately unimportant effort to identify which *specific* pieces of the hut's walls were set in place before which other ones and what the specific relationship of any of those pieces might be to the ones that preceded them. To become entangled in that kind of fruitless pondering is almost certainly to skate past the two details that actually *are* at the heart of the matter: that the hut exists at all and that you have somehow been granted the right to dwell in it.

We often speak of the process of coming to know God, or even just to know *of* God, as a kind of journey. But this alternate metaphor, the one that features the seeker of God as living in an old *sukkah* rather than traveling along an ancient road, is just as valid and can function as an equally useful metaphor. Both have impeccable scriptural pedigrees as well: the psalmist quoted above who wrote of his longing to dwell in God's house forever (Psalm 27:4) is no more or less right than the one who prayed that God would make clear "the path wherein I should walk" (Psalm 143:8).

EMBRACING PARADOX

God is everything and nothing, in every place without exception and in no place that exists according to the physics of the world. God belongs to the world and is other than the world . . . and is therefore the definition of absolute existence that does not exist at all or, more precisely, that cannot be said to exist without that declaration impacting fatally on any human-brain-based conception regarding the nature of existence. These paradoxes are riddles, not falsehoods. And they are the platform on which must stand all who would know God without ruining their efforts with even the least apparently consequential lie.

For Jewish souls, the journey to God will almost always be imagined as a road paved with the commandments of the Torah, but those very laws will serve collectively as a great impediment in the path of any who seek communion with the divine realm absent an abiding commitment to absolute intellectual and spiritual integrity. More than slightly paradoxically, however, those same laws *also* serve as the absolutely indispensable tools all must learn to wield who would devote their lives to the cultivation of such a communion experience by embracing the notion that God may be known through obedience, fealty, submission and allegiance.

The truly righteous in the world know these truths, yet somehow *also* find themselves able to listen to the soundless voice of the living God they know they know and they know they do not—and will not ever—know . . . and, in so doing, to attempt to gaze upon the divine face—which possibility the psalmist certified as real with the words, "Justified finally, I shall gaze on Your face (Psalm 17:16)"—at the same time they accept—and accept totally and without reservation—that it is impossible to see the face of God and survive the experience "for none can see Me and live" (Exodus 33:20).

God is the fullness of the world, such that there is no place devoid of divine reality. But even though this concept has stirred creative hearts for millennia, it is nonetheless totally beyond human comprehension—and also so completely and absolutely self-evident as to be more or less axiomatic for those who decide to spend their lives seeking out communion with the divine in accordance with the prophet's sacred injunction, "Seek God and live!" (Amos 5:6).

The author of the 119th psalm expressed the same truth when he wrote of himself, "I have sought You with all my heart" (Psalm 119:10), thus presenting the totality of his credo in three simple Hebrew words and challenging his readers to follow his exalted lead by undertaking a journey to God that involves burrowing as deeply as possible into the inmost chambers of a heart that contains and cannot possibly contain a glimmer of the perceptible spark of divinity that the universe itself contains and cannot possibly hold, and which must be and cannot be part of God.

From the effort expended honestly to embrace mutually exclusive ideas about God as self-evident truths, all of which must be true and none of which can be true, can come the energy able to move us forward toward the great goal of knowing the God who exists enshrouded in an opaque cloud of unknowing and also available to all who have the courage to open their eyes and to see the Creator's light glimmering behind the opacity of the created world.

DENOUNCING SUPERSTITION

For Jewish people, the path that leads toward a life in God will be paved with the commandments, but these commandments are neither magic rituals that have the power to elicit God's blessings nor superstitious rites that have any effect of any sort on the world other than the one they have on worshipers seeking to elevate their souls through submission to the covenant and its codicils. This lesson is at the core of the biblical injunction to know God through divine service and, indeed, when the text mysteriously notes that the Israelites of old were commanded to cleave unto God, the very next verse hones that point forcefully by presenting God pausing to explain how such a thing could be possible: "For," God says, "behold, I have taught you My laws and statutes" (Deuteronomy 4:4–5). It is thus through faithful allegiance to the terms of the covenant, Scripture is teaching, that communion with God may effectively be sought even today by the descendants of those Israelites to whom God spoke the commandments aloud at Sinai. But what is true for the men and women of the House of Israel is also true for all of God's creatures: to exist in a state of obedient submission to the terms of a covenant forged with God requires obedience, submission . . . and a covenant forged with God. For the men and women of the House of Israel, that covenant will always be the Torah itself. But each nation has the ability and the right to forge its own covenant with God, one reflective of its own unique relationship with the God of all nations. Because God is the moral core of the world, all such covenants forged in good faith and honestly will be elaborations of the same moral code. The details will differ. But the set of core concepts that underlie those details will reflect the simple fact that, in the end, there is only one God.

THE WIDE HEART

The foundational idea of Scripture is that allegiance to the covenant—which the Bible understands to constitute the specific form submission to the will of God takes when translated from theory into practice—can make the heart wide enough and deep enough to contain some immeasurably small spark of the divine spirit. Indeed, it is precisely this experience of opening up the inmost chambers of the secret heart to the palpable, dynamic presence of God that defines the experience of cleaving unto God and makes of it the great and noble goal of all human spiritual endeavor.

This point permeates biblical thinking about God, even when it is not made explicit. For example, consider two adjacent verses in the 119th psalm. In the first, the poet writes personally and says, "I have cleaved unto Your testimonies, O God" (Psalm 119:31). And the verse that follows explains how this works: "I run [toward You] along the path of Your commandments [and I succeed when] You sufficiently widen my heart" (Psalm 119:32).

By juxtaposing his ideas in this specific way, the poet is saying two specific things. One is that spiritual and intellectual communion with God will come to most people as a function of the degree to which they have allowed themselves to commit to the performance of the commandments that Scripture presents as divine law. And the other is that such people alone will be possessed of sufficient spiritual force to widen the chambers of their human hearts to the degree necessary to allow the real, palpable presence of God to enter into its chambers. Historically speaking, this is the reason Jews have traditionally sought to cleave unto God by cleaving first unto the commandments of the Torah and it is also why they have traditionally referred to those commandments liturgically as "their lives and the length of their days" (Deuteronomy 30:20)—not because it is literally so, but because they possess the capability of leading flesh-and-blood individuals anchored to the world and its immutable physics to a life in God, who is the Life of the Universe and the divine Steward of its days.

The ancients attempted to describe this greatest of all spiritual goals along all sorts of mythic and poetic lines, including the famous description of the experience of opening the heart to the presence of God as a kind of surgical operation designed *actually* to widen the chambers of the human heart . . . as though the whole difficulty in cleaving unto God might literally be that the chambers of the average heart are simply too narrow to accommodate the divine spirit without somehow being made physically wider and deeper. Indeed, the addition to the daily prayer service of the short prayer attributed to the Talmudic sage Mar son of Rabina—words traditional Jewish worshipers even today recite three or four, sometimes even five, times in the course of a day—to the effect that what honest supplicants truly need from God is that the chambers of their hearts be made open to the Torah so that their souls might more actively pursue the performance of the commandments is merely the translation of this idea into the practical language of prayer.

In biblical times, this theoretical widening of the heart to the divine spirit was referred to as the circumcision of the heart, as in the verse from the tenth chapter of Deuteronomy that reads, "And you shall circumcise the foreskin of your heart" (Deuteronomy 10:16). The ancients, of course, did not imagine that *actual* surgery could possibly make it feasible for the divine spirit to enter into the hearts of people who would otherwise be unable to accommodate its presence. Rather, this was merely a poetic way of saying that the sole legitimate point of worship is to prepare the human heart for the entry of the spirit of the living God, that spark of divine reality to which the human soul may effectively cleave when it is perceptibly present within a person's breast and not merely within the confines of that individual's intellect as a lofty idea or a philosophical construct.

THE DIVINE IMAGE

The notion that mortal individuals can move toward attaining the great goal of integrating their spiritual selves—their souls—into God by observing even those divine laws that appear solely to be concerned with regulating behavior between earth-bound human beings is a cornerstone concept of biblical theology and a foundational idea of both ancient and modern Judaism. Indeed, the whole process of attempting to feel God's presence on earth through the pursuit of ever more moral and more decent interpersonal relationships is designed precisely to lead to what poets call the integration of the inner and outer self in God and what mystics call *d'veikut*, the act of cleaving unto God. And, indeed, most people take their first steps toward *d'veikut* precisely by turning to face an individual in the world other than themselves and then relating to that individual in a way that reflects their unshakable conviction that that person, by virtue of being a human being and in a way specifically unrelated to his or her behavior or moral bearing, is created in the image of God.

It sounds a lot easier than it is, especially when the people who cross our paths are not endowed with qualities reminiscent of God's grandeur or power on earth. It is not especially taxing, after all, to find traces of the Almighty in the physical presence of the strong and mightily powerful on earth, just as it is relatively simple to find traces of Judge God present in the physical presence of human judges as they preside over their courtrooms and pass judgment on the defendants who come before them. Less simple, however, will be finding the image of God stamped on poverty-stricken individuals struggling to keep from drowning in the circumstances of their own lives . . . and it is precisely for this reason that the Torah presents such a large number of laws rooted in the notion that it is an act of divine worship—and not merely an expression of natural kindness—to lift the indigent up out of poverty and to refuse *not* to listen to the cries of the needy when they call out in distress. Indeed, when the Bible declares that "those who stop up their ears to the cries of the needy will themselves not be answered when they cry out in need" (Proverbs 21:13), the meaning is simply that, just as we all have the ability to help or to refuse help to people who are needy in comparison to ourselves, so are all people needy and indigent in comparison to the Almighty, who will respond or decline to respond to our cries for help in times of trouble in direct relationship to the degree to which we have previously responded to the needs of those in our midst who have turned to us for assistance. In the end, human beings have the freedom to choose how to live in the world. But there is no more pathetic fantasy than the notion that the way we live in the world will not—or, even more perversely, cannot— have any influence on the degree to which we know God.

The act of seeking to cleave unto God by searching for the trace of divinity stamped on even the most miserable human beings is called "the sanctification of life" in the language of Scripture because those individuals who show mercy and kindness to others *because* of the trace of the divine image they perceive in even the least enviable of human beings are able—both in theory and in practice—to use the acts of succor and kindness they perform for those people to build a kind of bridge, physically unreal but also fully traversable, to the God whom Scripture acclaims over and over as the Holy One of Israel.

Therefore, all who do not pervert the justice due even to the least influential member of society—*and* who do not take the clothing of the poor as collateral when they lend them money and then keep the garments overnight instead of returning them by nightfall (Exodus 22:25–26) *and* who do not charge interest on such loans (Exodus 22:24, Leviticus 25:36–37, Deuteronomy 23:20–21) *and* who decline ever to oppress the strangers in their midst (Exodus 22:20 and 23:9), *and* who endeavor to make sure even orphans and strangers are properly represented in court when they are forced to seek redress for the legitimate grievances they have against people attempting to exploit them (Deuteronomy 24:17)—all such people are deemed by Scripture to have come one step closer to God through every single act of solicitude and caring they perform.

LIBERATION AND REDEMPTION

When the ancient poet wrote of himself that he was "imprisoned and unable to escape" (Psalm 88:9), he was not an actual prisoner in a real prison of some sort, but was merely commenting on the human condition and noting that we are, all of us, prisoners of our own moral deficiencies, ethical inadequacies, and spiritual shortcomings. That particular poet lived in ancient times, but the truth behind his poem is as evident today as it ever was. Most human beings, after all, do not live in real jails with bars across the windows and high walls at the perimeter of the property, but the prisons we moderns inhabit—ones in which we are held in place by our own boorishness, selfishness, and oafishness—are nevertheless fully real.

This notion—that all people are prisoners in prisons that they themselves have built—is a basic principle. But there is another that needs to be paired with it: the notion that God has the power, the ability, and the will to free the incarcerated from even the most escape-proof of such prisons. Liberation from the world of inadequacy and ethical flaw is called redemption, which can then be defined as the loosening of the bonds of shortcoming that plague us all as we struggle toward the great goal of living lives in God. Redemption, however, is a reward from God and this single notion—that we can be freed from the bonds that hold us back by embracing faith in God as the Author of liberation and freedom in the world at the same time we acknowledge that those bonds are wholly of our own fashioning—is one of the most basic and enduring principles of faith and, at that, the one that serves as the gateway through which all who serve as their own jailers, which is all of us, must pass to know God other than as mere theory or dogma.

DRINKING THE LIVING WATERS

Just as there is a "*torah* of truth" behind and beyond the parchment scroll Jews revere as *the* Torah, so is there a world behind and beyond the world we know and this world, in parallel fashion, in known as the "World of Truth." In other contexts, however, this World of Truth is also called the Kingdom of God or the World to Come, the latter of which names implies that it is the realm in which the faithful will surely come to know God *if* they manage to free their souls from the bonds imposed on them by the very nature of terrestrial existence by dedicating themselves to the service of God without surrendering to self-interest and by striving to live lives unsullied by sin.

This ability to encounter God in the world behind the world is said by Scripture to be the lot of the righteous, as in the verse from the 119th psalm that reads "God is my lot / I pledge to keep Your commands" (Psalm 119:57) or the one from the sixteenth psalm in which the poet plainly declares, "God is my portion, my lot" (Psalm 16:5). These verses are from different poems and were almost certainly written by different authors, but they point to a single truth: that the ability to cleave unto God is the lot—and the right—of all believers who yearn to serve and worship God wholeheartedly and without spoiling their own efforts by layering them over with selfishness or crippling delusions of self-importance. And this is also the meaning of the famous verse from Deuteronomy, "Moses has bequeathed us Torah as an inheritance for the congregation of Jacob" (Deuteronomy 33:4), which is to say: the Torah is the natural inheritance of all who cleave unto its commandments and attempt to walk in its ways, and so the natural lot and portion of the faithful. Regarding the wicked, on the other hand, Scripture declares that "the spirit of terror is the cup from which *they* drink" (Psalm 11:6). The use of this idea—that with our deeds we fashion the cup from which we then drink either the purest water or the bitterest gall—appears elsewhere in Scripture with respect to the pious in the verse that notes that God alone is the cup from which they drink the living waters of faith and, indeed, the end of the verse cited above from the sixteenth psalm makes that point explicitly as the poet addresses God and says simply, ."..You are my cup / the framer of my destiny" (Psalm 16:5).

ZION AND SINAI

The simplest test of the legitimacy of a given act of divine worship is whether it enables the individual performing it to move forward psychically, spiritually, and emotionally toward a state of ongoing communion and intimacy with God.

This truth is hidden just behind the famous words spoken by God to Abraham at the beginning of the twelfth chapter of Genesis: "Go forth from your country, from your homeland and from your father's house to the land that I shall show you" (Genesis 12:1). These words were addressed to Abraham when he was in Haran. But was Haran Abraham's homeland? Didn't Scripture note just a few lines earlier that Abraham's father Teraḥ "took his son Abram and his grandson Lot, Haran's son, and his daughter-in-law Sarai, the wife of Abram, and together with them set forth from Ur Kasdim to travel to the Land of Canaan but only got as far as Haran, where they ended up settling" (Genesis 11:31)? Behind this apparent inner-textual discrepancy, however, lies a profound lesson: by commanding Abraham to leave his homeland when he had already done so, the Torah is teaching us that it was not *only* from Mesopotamia to Israel that Abraham was being commanded to travel, but from the domain of the mundane to the domain of the sacred, from the everyday world of dust and mud to the realm of the holy, from the realm of mere existence to the Holy Land, to Jerusalem, to God.

And, indeed, God is acclaimed subtly but repeatedly throughout Scripture as the land in which the faithful dwell, as the land in which the patriarchs wandered and toward which pilgrims to this day still wander, as the fertile soil in which the spirit can grow to full maturity when an individual is wholly given over to the worship of God. It is for this reason that God is called Zion, as in the famous words of two prophets "For from Zion comes forth the Torah" (Isaiah 2:3 and Micah 4:2), in which "Zion" cannot possibly refer to Mount Zion in Jerusalem since the Torah was revealed to Israel at Mount Sinai and not in Jerusalem at all. But if it was *at* Sinai that the Torah was first revealed, it is nonetheless *from* God that it continues to be revealed as it inspires and directs the faithful toward the great goal of communion with the living spirit of the divine.

From all this, it follows that the faithful may profitably think of God as the vast land for which the pious yearn and in which they are called to spend the days of their lives attempting to settle. It is for this reason that so many Jewish sages have concluded from their study of Scripture that settling in the Land of Israel is one of the commandments of Scripture—not because the other lands of the globe are somehow less meaningfully part of God's creation, but simply because the act of traveling to Zion and settling there is meant to symbolize the willingness of an individual to undertake the long, protracted journey to spiritual fulfillment in God. And if a clever soul were to ask how, if God exists in every place, there can be any real spiritual advantage in living in one specific land or another, then the answer would have to be that those who travel to the Holy Land—and especially those who travel there with the express intention of settling there—elevate their souls to the Holy One of Israel by seeking holiness in a land that is wholly holy, in a land suffused by God with the sanctity of the divine.

THE PROPHETS' TORAH

It is entirely natural for people to imitate their own past behavior and to walk the most comfortably along paths they themselves have already at least once followed, and this is implied in the famous statement of Ben Azzai's mentioned above (and preserved in the Mishnah at M. Avot 4:2) to the effect that the reward of performing one of the commandments is the energy and inclination to undertake the performance of another and that, similarly, the freedom to sin is engendered more than by anything else by the knowledge that one has *already* sinned and, as sinners like to think, gotten away with it.

The prophets of Israel, however, had their own *torah*, according to which the reward inherent in the performance of a commandment of Scripture is the slow integration of the soul of the worshiper into the great ocean of perceptible/imperceptible reality that is God's presence in the mundane world. According to this model, the reward for the performance of a commandment is that the individual in question personally becomes one of a series of never ending, permanently undulating waves that do and cannot exist as they flourish within the ocean of exalted reality and absolute unreality that is God's dwelling place in a world that both does and cannot contain even the smallest spark of God's ultimate reality.

STANDING ON YOUR OWN SHOULDERS

The concept of attempting to see further by standing on your own shoulders, the notion of coming to accept principles that you find implausible or improbable by embracing them both tentatively *and* wholeheartedly, the idea of taking your first truly productive, meaningful steps forward on the path to spiritual wholeness by first spending years on the same road you are about to travel . . . these paradoxes are all the natural results of the attempt of the individual possessed of spiritual integrity creatively, productively, and intelligently to exploit the tension that results from undertaking tasks that are achievable and unachievable at the same time . . . and to use the energy that derives from the tension between possibility and impossibility to unravel the riddle of seeking to know a God whom reason and logic dictate must be considered wholly unknowable. This is the inner meaning of the verse from the Torah, "Serve God and cleave unto God" (Deuteronomy 10:20), which is to say: cleave unto God by means of worship, for you will never succeed in knowing God unless you first find the strength to approach in worshipful dialogue a God you have yet to know or regarding whose existence you have yet to feel totally secure and unconflicted . . . despite the fact that it is not actually possible to engage in dialogue at all with an unknown and silent partner, let alone to do so in the context of the reverence due God.

WHAT THE FAITHFUL ALREADY KNOW

God is neither from the world nor of the world, but neither is God to be found in some hidden crevice of being behind or beneath or beyond the world, and this in turn is the meaning of the passage in the book of the prophet Hosea that reads, "For I am God and not a [mere] mortal, the Holy One in your midst" (Hosea 11:9). Indeed, God is found in no place and in every place, and was therefore known to the sages of classical antiquity as the Place . . . because, as repeatedly noted above, even though the world is not the place of God, God may still somehow be described aptly as the Place of the World.

God is not the whole world or even a part of it, but is rather the knowable/unknowable Soul of the universe and its Heart. To seek God in the context of worship, however, is not impossible. Nor is the struggle to do so an exercise in irrationality, sublime or otherwise. Yet, to attempt to journey toward faith in the context of unwavering spiritual integrity, would-be pilgrims on their way to Jerusalem must embrace several ideas that will require more than just casual effort to accept wholeheartedly. For example, such tentative pilgrims will have to accept

- that there is reasonability in seeking communion with the divine in a world that cannot logically or reasonably contain God,
- that faith, no matter how pure, will always be ruined when used as a shield against truth, most definitely including scientific truth, and
- that the pilgrim following along on the path to Jerusalem must agree to seek God in places God cannot logically exist—and to do so without despairing or succumbing to the almost overwhelming temptation to fashion a spiritual life based on lies or half-truths.

Scripture uses the Hebrew word *rasha* to categorize the individual who lies about God. The term, literally meaning "villain" or "wicked person," seems harsh, yet this is precisely the truth that emerges from a consideration of two verses in the Book of Isaiah. The first ordains people yearning for God to "seek God where God may be found" (Isaiah 55:6). That sounds encouraging enough, but then the prophet moves forward and, lest seekers fall prey to their own fantasies, prays that "the *rasha* abandon his wicked way and the iniquitous individual, his wicked thoughts" (Isaiah 55:7). In other words, seek God where God may be found: in the labyrinthine matrices of an intellect unsullied by willingly embraced falsehood, self-serving fantasy, or even the most flattering of lies about God. God surely may be found, the prophet is saying—but not in any of those places!

IS THERE NO GOD IN ISRAEL?

Somehow, the ancient prohibition of seeking God through the medium of idolatrous worship has ended up in the modern world translated into a general ill ease about seeking real, content-rich communion with God at all. This is not entirely illogical—it was, after all, content-rich communion with God that the idolaters of old too were seeking—but embracing idolatry is as grave a misstep as any could be for the pilgrim seriously interested in using the rituals of religion to embrace not *only* theoretical faith in God's existence, but a real sense of God's palpably real presence in the world. Therefore, although it is forbidden—and forbidden absolutely—to seek communion with Baal-Zebub (as indicated by the sarcastic question the angel bid the prophet Elijah put to the messengers of King Ahaziah at 2 Kings 1:3: "Go up to the messengers of the king of Samaria and say unto them, 'Is there no God in Israel that you are constrained to seek communion with Baal-Zebub, the god of Ekron?'"), it is entirely permitted to seek communion with the God of Israel and this is what the prophet Hosea meant when he declared his own day to be the right time to seek out God so that "God may come and teach . . . justice" (Hosea 10:12). It is also what the Torah means to teach us is permitted when it says of Rebecca that "she went to seek communion with God" (Genesis 25:22), thus saying almost clearly that she neither sought advance permission from the religious authorities of her day nor took the time to earn an advanced degree in theology before setting forth, but instead approached God possessed solely of her own spiritual probity and intellectual integrity . . . and that that that was more than enough for God to look with favor on her efforts and to speak to her directly and clearly.

The bottom line is that all who teach that seeking communion with God is impossible are denying both the point of religion and the accessible reality of God in the world. Do lovers somehow debase the purity of their passion by seeking to translate it from the realm of unfulfilled pining into the sphere of ongoing dialogue and physically real pleasure by actually encountering each other in the world? Who would wish to argue *that* point?

MORE THAN SELF-PRESERVATION

Religion at its best is far more of a construction site than an art gallery. As a result, the pious individual should act far less like the curator of a gallery of sacred things and far more like a millworker willing and ready to take the rules and rituals of faith and transform them into useful planks with which to construct a traversable bridge that not only exists in sublime theory, but that can actually support flesh-and-blood men and women seeking to cross over it as they make their progress forward toward recognizable and attainable spiritual goals.

Within the Jewish world, Jewish continuity—the successful passing of the Torah to the next generation—is often touted as the great challenge facing the current generation of Jewish people. (I suppose this idea must be part of other faith groups' self-conception as well, but here again I write of what I know.) The idea has a certain appealing ring to it (because, in the end, what group wishes to think of itself as traveling the road to its own extinction), but the great goal of Jewish life cannot merely be to stave off its own disappearance. Rather, the whole point of preserving Jewish life is to give into the hands of the Jews of a new generation the possibility of unifying the name of God through the performance of the commandments and, in so doing, to cleave unto God personally and meaningfully. The irony here, of course, is that the successful effort to depict religion as the context, not for the performance of countless ritual tasks and the recitation of even less countable numbers of prayers, but for real, measurable growth toward a clearly defined spiritual goal that utilizes those rituals and prayers as a mean unto an end rather than as ends unto themselves—the successful depiction of religion as the context for that kind of real growth is precisely what *would* guarantee the appeal of any religion to a new generation of potential adherents.

REPENTANCE

God functions in the universe as the ordering force that rests just behind, beneath, and behind every physically existent thing, and also as the ontological energy that enables those things to bear existence in real space. Therefore, any who seek to live in a state of ongoing communion with God must learn to transcend the boundaries of the world and, in so doing, to come to a place that exists without any trace of physicality, to a place that is and is not part of the world, to a place that exists solely as creative, poetic energy, to a place that is the Place of the World without the world actually being its place . . . but none of this will ever be possible for prisoners of the world who are incarcerated in its physics in the way actual prisoners in jail are kept in place by bars of steel.

Since God is totally other than the created universe, it follows that human beings can only discern the divine in the universe they inhabit through the media of allusive hint and indirect suggestion. Nonetheless, the ancients believed that God could be seen in their world as a shadow of emergent luminescence that occasionally shone forth from deep within the Holy of Holies, the experience of which light the psalmist daringly referenced as salvation itself, as in the famous verse: "Shine the light of Your face upon Your servant / grant me salvation according to Your great mercy" (Psalm 31:17). Even those few who knew how to look in precisely the right direction at precisely the right moment saw almost nothing, however—"for none can see Me and live" (Exodus 33:20)—but they still maintained a serious advantage over those who looked in the wrong direction at the right time or *vice versa*, or, needless to say, those who looked in the wrong direction at the wrong moment. Those in the final category, of course, were doomed to see nothing at all. But even those in the first didn't see much. The Holy of Holies, of course—once the inmost sanctum of the Jerusalem Temple—has not existed in real space for almost two millennia. Yet the light of God's presence endures in the world nonetheless for those who know where to look and how to seek it out.

The goal of Judaism is to turn the Jew toward God and it is for this reason that the effort to establish a life of communion with God is called by the name *t'shuvah*. Although generally translated with the English word "repentance," *t'shuvah* is not at all the same thing as regret or remorse, and refers—at least when used to describe spiritual potential—to the actual decision to turn toward the light of God's face. This is what was meant when, speaking through the prophet Ezekiel, God commanded the people to "turn and live" (Ezekiel 18:32)—which is to say: *turn* to face Me and, if you can summon up the requisite amount of spiritual energy, *live* with Me in a state of ongoing psychic communion.

JOY AND INTEGRITY

When Scripture ordains that worshipers approach the divine palace in joy, as, for example, in the words cited earlier of the one hundredth psalm, "Serve ye God in joy" (Psalm 100:2), the concept is that the supplicant before God is not meant to be alienated or depressed by worship—both of which are natural responses to acknowledging God as the wholly Other. But equally important is that the worshiper not misconstrue this obligation to worship joyfully as some sort of tacit permission to seek joy in the realm of illusory fantasy. Just to the contrary is the case, in fact: the injunction to worship in joy is meant to remind those who seek God in the world that it is possible, and eminently so, to suffuse worshipful activity with deep meaning, honest emotion, and sincere longing to the extent that those efforts succeed at creating the kind of deep inner joy that comes from being at peace with the world . . . and with yourself.

Hiding behind the psalmist's almost simple injunction to serve God joyfully, however, is the corollary notion that all who would aspire to the worship of God in joy should feel grateful that they are able to know joy in this sorry world at all. This challenge was not unknown to the ancients who found in their experience of the divine the source of joy in the world, as the author of the fourth psalm wrote, "You have placed joy in my heart" (Psalm 4:8), but who *also* needed to struggle through the paradox that the joy worshipers are called upon to bring to their service is *itself* a gift of God. Worshipers must therefore *be* joyful because they have come closer to God through the medium of rite, ritual, and prayer, but also aware enough of how things are in the world to find in God the source of that same joy. This strange, slightly impossible notion—that joy is both the most basic element the worshiper must bring to worship and also the great reward bestowed on the worshiper as God's response to those same worshipful acts—will be easier to fathom when compared to the acts that characterize the love relationship between human partners at its most transcendent. Indeed, the sublime gifts lovers offer each other to create their relationship in the first place—passion, vulnerability, desire, respect, affection, and friendly acceptance untainted by judgmentalism or preconception—those gifts are precisely the ones most perceive to result *from* the successful engagement of another in the context of love. This should logically be impossible, at least for lovers anchored to the inexorable flow of time from the past into the future. And yet the love of lovers is somehow possible nonetheless . . . and so is worship undertaken with a willing spirit and a joyful heart.

THE TRIPLE TORAH

No Jewish reader will find the assertion that the Torah is at the heart of Jewish life at all surprising or debatable. But saying how that works—in other words, how precisely an ancient book can function in the modern world as an ongoing source of sufficient spiritual energy to propel those who cling fast to it forward on a lifelong journey to the attainment of specific spiritual goals—*that* will be significantly more challenging for most. One way to approach the issue could lie in imagining the Torah to be possessed of three basic aspects, each parallel to a specific counterpart in human life.

The human being appears before the world in three basic guises: as the clothed individual visible to any casual passerby, as the body of flesh and blood beneath the clothing that only an individual's most intimate friends and lovers ever see, and as the soul that animates and inspires the living person that no one ever sees and which, consequently, none can damage or attack—but which *also* constitutes the inmost and most private iteration of that person's self and thus the part with which someone in love with that individual wants the most ardently to engage. That much seems obvious enough. But seizing the relation between these three aspects of human existence can lead to a way of understanding how the word of the living God, encapsulated and presented to humankind in the Torah millennia ago, can still function in the real world as a framework for meaningful spiritual growth.

Similar to the way the human body exists in the world in the three specific guises mentioned above, the Torah also has three existential aspects.

The most basic aspect of the Torah is the scroll called "The Written Torah" by our ancient sages. It is revelation translated into the domain of parchment and ink, the communicative presence of the divine encapsulated in the sounds and utterances of written and spoken language. As such, it is available to all, which is what Scripture means when it refers to itself as "the Torah that Moses set before Israel" (Deuteronomy 4:44), that is to say: before all Israel with no exceptions at all.

More interior than that is the aspect of commandment and law that has its origins in the notion that God may be known not merely through intellectualizing, but through physical service. These commandments are included in the written Torah, but they are distinct from it as well—the act of eating *matzah* at Passover is not to be confused with the passage in the Torah ordaining the eating of *matzah* at Passover, nor is it to be assumed that the possibility of spiritual advancement that derives from eating *matzah* at the appointed time in the course of a specific festival will necessarily be the same as the advancement that derives from studying the passage in Scripture that commands that *matzah* be eaten at the appointed time.

Most interior of all are the secrets and mysteries that surround even the most apparently ordinary section of Scripture. These esoteric interpretations are the province of scholars possessed of the ability to pierce through both text and ritual to see beneath the surface of both and to understand how the two intertwine to create the context for attaining a level of intimacy with the divine realm.

Attaining the first level, the level of study of the written word of Scripture, is an act of respect toward the presence of God on earth. Attaining the second level, the level of practice and observance, is an act of fealty, devotion, and submission. Attaining the third aspect, the level of knowing the Torah not according to the garments it wears in the world or the rituals it inspires but rather according to rules of its inmost sphere, the realm in which dwell its most recondite secrets—that is the true love of God to which all are called by Scripture but not all ever attain. But for all this third level is often dismissed, albeit deferentially, as the province of mystics and saints, the truth is that the third level is attainable—and wholly so—by all who devote themselves to the quest for God in the world through the informed excavation of the human soul, through prayer, and through contemplative, intelligent introspection infused with the unyielding commitment to intellectual and emotional integrity. Again, the parallel to the search for love is pertinent. Not all can write poetry or compose long songs worthy of the name. Not all are sufficiently articulate to focus their yearning and intense desire for another through the prism of spoken language. Not all can afford the kind of gifts for a beloved that by their opulence suggest the depth of passion in the giver's heart. But the ability *itself* to love—and to experience the deep passion and intense pleasure that loving another entails—*that* ability inheres in the human condition itself deeply and elementally, and entirely independently of any individual's ability to express the emotions that ability inspires in any specific way.

SEEKERS AFTER GOD

Although the notion that God is the Creator of the world and the Author of existence is the basic building block of faith, it is also a slippery concept that even the *most* pious find difficult to seize totally . . . and how much the more so average people who are attempting to find faith in God the Creator at the same time they grapple with the misery and suffering of the people who actually live in Creator God's created world. Such people are called in Scripture "seekers after God" (as, for example, in the eleventh verse of the thirty-fourth psalm) because, although they *wish* to believe and *exert* themselves to believe, they have not yet come to the point at which they actually *do* believe in God in the normal way people believe in the unconditional, unquestionable existence of the things they see around them. In a way, such people are the latter-day counterparts of the ancient pilgrims who made their slow progress to Jerusalem three times a year, traveling step by step along the dusty pathways of ancient Israel but who, until they actually stood in the gates of the Holy City, were able only to *hope* that they would eventually arrive at their chosen destination.

Scripture does not look down on such travelers merely because they are traveling to a destination they have yet to reach, opting instead to praise them for being on a journey to a sacred destination in the first place. And it was precisely in that spirit that the poet whose poem became the 100th psalm called out to the pilgrims of his own day as they made their way toward Jerusalem with the words, "Come to its gates imbued with a spirit of thanksgiving, to its courtyards with the praise of God on your lips" (Psalm 100:4). And what words follow in the psalm almost immediately? "For God is good and divine mercy is forever / faith in God abides for all time" (Psalm 100:5), that is to say: the reward stored up for the intrepid pilgrims of *any* generation who advance toward the gates of Jerusalem one step at a time is faith in the God of *all* generations, that same God who patiently waits for the pilgrims of every generation to make their way from the mundane world to the realm of holiness along the path trod for them by the righteous of earlier generations, the path of gracious and heartfelt fidelity to the Torah and willing submission to its moral precepts, ethical values, ritual requirements, and eternal standards of behavior.

THE LANGUAGE OF THE SPIRIT

Just as water requires some sort of container to transcend *mere* existence and actually to become useful to someone attempting to bring it home from the well, so do thoughts require to be set into words if they are to transcend the boundaries of the creative consciousness and exist in a practical, useful way to other people in the world. Indeed, this ability to transform thoughts from ideas that roil and smolder in the inmost chambers of the heart into transmissible concepts that can be shared with others is among the greatest of God's gifts and so is King Solomon cited in Scripture as saying specifically that "the panoply of [thoughts that reside deep within the human] heart may belong to the individual, but [the ability to share them with others through the use of] language is a gift from God" (Proverbs 16:1).

The commandments of the Torah are words in the language of the spirit, that language of desire in which even the most intimate thoughts that develop within an individual's creative spiritual consciousness can find expression. And the king's observation about language applies here as well: the ability to express the most profound longing for God through the wordless language of ritual and rite is itself best understood as a gift from God—and, at that, one capable of binding the faithful below to their divine Parent no less securely and meaningfully than their ability to speak binds them to their neighbors and relations. Moreover, just as the words of any given terrestrial language are totally artificial in the sense that there is no real relationship of any sort between the words in a specific language and the things of the world designated by those words (and examples of onomatopoeia are merely the handful of exceptions that prove the general rule), so are the commandments of Scripture artificial in the sense that there is no real, empirically provable or demonstrable relationship between God and the deeds human beings undertake to give physical expression to their longing for God. However, just as no reasonable person would respond to the realization that language is artificial by refusing on principle to speak at all, so should no one possessed of real spiritual goals respond to the realization that the commandments are merely "words" by means of which longing for God can find expression in the physical world by refusing to perform them.

This point is key. As a working rabbi, I have occasionally encountered people who justify their lack of fealty to Torah law with reference to the artificial nature of the commandments. To make that argument, however, is to miss the point almost entirely. Language is artificial, yet we all speak. Religion is artificial too, but it possesses the ability to allow us to speak to God and to hear God speak to us in return. That the constructs it calls into being as the framework for this kind of ongoing dialogue is not one that features wholly natural phenomena is true but irrelevant. Nor should this be an obscure point in need of longwinded explanation: if an individual can get past the fact that there is no organic link between words and things for long enough to order a toasted bagel in a coffee shop, then that same person should be able to get past the artificiality of religion long enough to utter a word in prayer or to do one of the commandments.

MAN, WOMAN, AND NATION

To speak in specifically Jewish terms, there surely is a certain basic contradiction between, on the one hand, the notion that the Torah exists to bind the members of the covenanted community together in common purpose so that they can pursue the worship of God as an aggregate of individuals who support and encourage each other and, on the other, the notion that that same religion exists for the specific purpose of enabling individuals to pursue their private, idiosyncratic, utterly *personal* paths forward toward the great goal of communion with God.

This paradox is not a feature solely of religious life, however, but will be familiar to all as a feature also of the relationship of citizen and citizenry in the context of public life: just as the citizens of a nation exist both as part of the national populace but also as individuals possessed of specific rights and privileges, so do those wholly devoted to the service of God exist as part of a huge nation of like-minded co-religionists devoted to the worship of God at the same time that they function as lonely pilgrims making their personal progress along lonesome paths that lead solely to private Jerusalems. Both are necessary. And, indeed, those who allow their national or ethnic identity to overwhelm their personal sense of themselves as solitary pilgrims seeking their way to the knowledge of God are no better off than those who allow their idiosyncratic search for personal redemption to weaken, or perhaps even in the extreme case to dissolve, their sense of themselves as part of a nation of co-religionists seeking God with shared resolve and a deep, abiding sense of common purpose.

THE POSSIBLE/IMPOSSIBLE JOURNEY

The great journey to God is both the experience depicted symbolically by the ancients as a journey to the divine palace in heaven and, at the same time, also a trip to the inmost chambers of the human heart. These two symbolic ranges are actually two sides of the same sacred coin, however, because traveling the road to God requires, first of all, learning how to descend to the very depths of your own perceptive consciousness and there, in the deepest recesses of introspective self-awareness charged with electrified spiritual longing, to find the very beginning—and also the end—of the long path that leads to Jerusalem, to God.

Therefore, those who are scrupulous in their obedience to the commandments not out of a sense of haughtiness toward the less punctiliously observant, but rather out a deep and abiding sense of love *for* God and awe *before* God—what such people get for their efforts is the ability to take a first step on the journey that will lead them to the depths of their own intuitive selves and to find there the possibility of personal redemption. Such people's devotion to the minutiae of religious observance is praiseworthy and admirable because it is rooted in their desire to know *of* God and to travel the sacred path that leads to spiritual wholeness *in* God.

However, there are also those whose scrupulous observance is essentially motivated by pride in their own religious zeal. Such people are careful in their observance *not* in order to pierce through the fog that surrounds the spark of the divine that smolders at the core of human consciousness, but rather in order to win the admiration and approval of their neighbors and friends. Theirs is the path that the psalmist called the "not good path" (Psalm 36:5), the path that leads nowhere at all.

Faith rooted in absolute spiritual integrity is not for the fainthearted, the weak-willed, or the uncertain. It is not something to be appreciated from a distance or taken out from time to time to be admired. It is the context in which human beings may reasonably yearn for redemption and, in the ultimate sense, it is the love of God translated into the language of human life. Like love in any context, it is fragile and substantial at the same time—capable of enduring the most grievous hardships, yet dissolvable—and irrevocably so—in lies and willfully self-induced delusions, no matter how piously framed or reverentially expressed.

Nothing is simpler than lying about God. But, for all tall tales may be temporarily soothing to the tormented, nothing is more detrimental to the human soul casting about in the world in search of deliverance than the telling of falsehoods, even intensely flattering ones, about God. And embracing *that* truth is the first step along the road to redemption, a road characterized both by the integrity of its milestones and by its possible-impossible ability to lead those who wander it possessed of yearning for heaven unsullied by arrogance and egotism to live lives in and of God, to find God, to be redeemed in God and, yes, ultimately, to know God. May such be the lot of us all!

Afterword

Once upon a time, a prince sent letters to a princess from a distant land of whom he had heard, but whom he had not ever actually met, and received letters back from her at regular intervals. As long as the prince remembered that the mental image of the princess that he saw in his mind's eye—and which he deeply cherished in his heart—was not the princess's real face, but rather a mental image that existed solely as a kind of self-generated commentary on the qualities and attributes of the princess he himself discerned from remarks and comments in her various letters, he was able to feel sure he would not be disappointed when they finally did manage to meet . . . because disappointment is nothing other than the inner response of the human heart to a sudden, unexpected lack of agreement between fantasy and reality and can, therefore, be effectively staved off by knowing better than to confuse the two.

The most important detail for the prince was to remember always that the actual way the princess looked was unrelated—and unrelated absolutely—both to the ability of his own imagination to conceive of her as looking one way or another in his waking or nighttime dreams . . . and also to the way her face seemed to him to be reflected in his tears of frustration and unsatisfied longing. She was a totally independent from the prince . . . at the same time that she was, somehow, part of him. She lived outside his world, but she also lived in it and, in a certain sense, in him. And although they were separated by thousands of miles, it was the purity of his longing—and its unyielding, unwavering integrity—that enabled the prince to live life as though theirs was the kind of love that could be had merely for the asking and, in so doing, to find comfort and true solace in hoping sincerely and even reasonably that they might one day meet and come to know each other intimately.

Maintaining this level of personal integrity was key, because then—and only then—did the possibility exist that the princess might someday honor his feelings and reciprocate his yearning and requite his passion . . . and that, some day in the future, she might agree to leave her distant castle to wed the prince who, at that point, will have spent a lifetime longing for her and who, on that day, will continue to love her with perfect honesty and total, unyielding commitment.

List of Abbreviations

M.	Mishnah
T.	Tosefta
B.	Babylonian Talmud
Y.	Yerushalmi (also known as the Palestinian Talmud)

Index

arrogance, 6, 11, 14, 23–24, 25, 51, 56, 71, 78, 94, 95, 102, 105–106, 113, 129, 159
autonomy: of God, 76; of humankind, 125
awe. *See* trembling, awe, and dread

beholdenness. *See* gratitude
belief. *See* faith
Beth-el. *See* Jacob's ladder
Bible: critical theories regarding, 47; fundamentalist approaches to, 36, 37, 38, 93; historicity of narrative, 48–49; literalist reading of, 48–49, 93; misuse of, 95; original language of, 44–45; public reading of, 71; relationship to *midrash*, 3, 52; relationship to mythology, 20, 51–52; study of, 53–54
biblical personalities: Abihu, 102; Abraham, 10–11, 99, 115–116, 133, 147; Adam and Eve, 60–61, 81, 124; Ahab, 4; Ahaziah, 150–151; David, 82, 99, 104, 127, 132, 133; Elijah, 106, 150–151; Ezra, 124; Hosea, 65, 149, 151; Isaiah, 13, 69, 92, 150; Jacob, 64–65, 84; Micaiah, 4; Moses, 14, 30, 37, 41, 42, 48, 49, 51, 54, 64, 67, 100, 116, 147, 154; Nadab, 102; Nehemiah, 124–125, 127; Pharaoh (of Exodus story), 31, 98; Pharaoh's daughter, 30; Samson, 12; Solomon, 48, 97, 100, 104; Zophar the Naamathite, 13, 14
blasphemy, viii, 39, 61, 113, 121–122, 130

commandments, 4, 16–20, 25–26, 29–31, 33–34, 38, 42, 53, 56–59, 61, 64–86, 90–104, 107–108, 110–112, 114–116, 120–121, 123–124, 126–128, 132, 134–136, 139, 141–144, 146, 148, 151, 154, 157–158; no definitive list of, 99–100; positive and negative, 107–108; rewards for the performance of, 65, 66, 70–71, 78, 113–115, 120, 127–128, 132–133, 146, 148–149, 153, 156
communion. *See d'veikut*.
covenant, 75, 95, 96, 108, 113, 116, 142, 143, 157

d'rishat ha-elohim ("seeking out God"), 27
d'veikut ("communion"), ix, x, 7, 27, 29, 31, 38, 39, 41, 43, 47, 48, 56, 65, 66, 68, 69, 71, 76, 91, 94–95, 96, 98, 103, 111, 116, 120–121, 123, 126, 128, 129, 131, 133, 139, 141–144, 147, 148, 150–153, 157–158
diaspora, 85, 87
dietary laws, 92, 134
dirshuni vi-ḥ'yu (Amos 5:4), 70, 74, 80
dread. *See* trembling, awe, and dread

emunah ("faith"). *See* faith
Eretz Yisrael. *See* Israel as the Holy Land
evil, 13, 28, 32; divine origin of, 13; and problem of theodicy, 70, 146–147, 150

165

exploitation of the commandments for personal gain, 93, 94–95

faith, viii–x, 4, 6, 7, 9–12, 15, 17–21, 23–34, 35–36, 38, 39, 46, 56, 58, 63, 70, 74, 77–80, 85, 86, 91, 92, 94, 106, 110, 112–115, 118–120, 122, 125–127, 129, 135, 137–138, 140, 146, 147, 149–151, 155–156, 159; as a bridge to God, 10, 19, 28–29
festivals, Jewish, 92; Passover, 30, 46, 101, 155; Sukkot, 80; Yom Kippur (Day of Atonement), 108
Foundation Stone, 135
fundamentalism, 36, 38–39, 93

God: as Author of History, 32, 33; as divine Friend, 81, 134; as divine Parent, 112, 117–118, 127, 138, 157; existence of outside of human ken, 15, 19, 20; existence of outside of space, 21, 27, 66, 84, 105, 106, 128; existence of outside of time, 14, 21, 27, 66, 84, 105, 106, 128; hearing, 40–41; as Heart of the World, 18, 134–135, 137; as heavenly Sovereign, 20–21, 39, 77, 84, 133, 158; humanity created in image of, 32, 79, 91, 96–97, 112, 123–124, 138, 139, 144–145; judgment by, 18, 60, 133, 144; knowing and knowing of, 2, 5–8, 11, 15, 19, 20, 41, 53, 64, 81, 90, 93–94, 100, 118, 128, 130, 136, 137, 142, 149, 158; language of, 7–8, 44–45, 77–78, 156–157; and light, 13, 14–15; as the moral core of being, 4, 85, 142; name of, 4, 7, 10, 38, 39, 40, 41, 54, 58, 59, 61, 67–68, 81, 91, 109–110, 114–115, 120, 137, 151; omnipotence of, 32, 33, 121–122; omniscience of, 26, 32, 33; perfection of, 75, 86, 90; as Place of the World, 20, 140, 149, 152; praying to, 16, 55–61, 70–72, 77, 87, 91, 106–107, 115, 117, 134, 138, 143–144, 153, 155, 157; serving, 77, 80, 84, 102–103, 113–114, 115, 132–133, 146, 158; submission to, 16, 75–77, 81, 87, 89–91, 93–94, 96–98, 100–103, 109–110, 113, 118, 123–125, 139, 141, 142–143, 155, 156; as Will of the World, 105; worshiping, 10, 12–13, 16, 17, 19, 26, 29–30, 58, 63–66, 69–87, 92–94, 97–99, 101–103, 108, 112–116, 120, 121, 124–125, 126, 128–129, 131, 134, 136, 138–139, 144, 145, 147–149, 153–154, 158. *See also* faith
gratitude, 12, 13, 110, 126–127

halakhah, 17
happiness and unhappiness, 13, 34, 81, 103–104
High Priest of Israel, 72, 96
holiness, 18, 38–39, 42, 45, 66–67, 89, 102–103, 106, 111, 121–123, 125–126, 135–136, 148, 156
Holocaust. *See* Shoah
honesty, viii, 3, 6–7, 10, 11, 18, 27, 33–34, 38, 56, 69, 93–94, 140–141
humankind: as God's partners in creation, 97–98. *See also* God, humanity created in image of
humility, 18, 45–46, 56, 58–59, 66, 110, 113, 115; and gullibility, 45–46; as antithesis to arrogance, 51

idolatry, 69–70, 150
integrity: intellectual, x, 38, 47, 140, 151; spiritual, ix, x, 6, 7–8, 11–15, 20, 33–34, 37, 40, 43, 56, 66, 67–68, 70–71, 80, 93–95, 102, 112, 115, 116, 119, 123, 125, 130, 141, 149, 150, 159
Israel as the Holy Land, 85, 96, 147, 148

Jacob's ladder, 64–65, 84
Jerusalem: gates of, 31, 100–101, 108, 156; as Holy City, 31, 85–86, 130, 135, 136, 156; pilgrimage to, 31, 85–86, 135–136; private version of, 15–16, 108, 158; walls of, 127
the Jewish people: commanded to be a holy people, 106; compared to sheep, 109–110. *See also* covenant
justice, 5–6, 82, 109, 110, 112–113, 118, 120, 121, 145, 151

Land of Israel. *See* Israel as the Holy Land
language, 28–29, 40, 49, 66, 98; as barrier, 106; of Bible, 44–45, 53; of God, 7–8;

inadequacy of, 12, 59–60, 65, 67, 123; as medium for communion, 35, 53, 54, 57–58, 77; as medium for prayer, 61, 87, 143–144, 155; of religion or spirituality, 9, 76, 156–157; of truth, 42. *See also* prayer, as bridge to God

loneliness, 119

love, 28, 30, 63, 72, 131–138, 153; of the commandments, 104; of God for humankind, 9, 11, 64, 81; of humankind for God, 2–4, 58, 79, 81, 86, 95, 111, 136, 155, 158, 159; possible/impossible nature of, 27, 72; relationship to worship, 63; romantic, 2, 7, 14, 16, 57, 63; source in God, 18

lying, viii, 5, 27, 94, 95, 150, 159; about God, viii, 5, 6, 8, 12, 14, 24, 33, 67, 130, 140, 150, 159; about religion, the Bible, and the history of religion, 6, 37, 38, 51, 74, 150. *See also* blasphemy

Mekhilta of Rabbi Ishmael, 26, 101, 114

melancholy, 34, 81

mishnaic and talmudic sages: Antigonos of Sokho, 65, 132; Ben Azzai, 71, 83, 148; Rabbi Aḥa bar Yaakov, 98; Rabbi Akiba, 32; Rabbi Ami, 140; Rabbi Eleazar, 132; Rabbi Eliezer, 102; Rabbi Hamnuna, 100; Rabbi Ḥanina, 8; Rabbi Josiah, 101; Rabbi Judah ben Tema, 101; Rabbi Judah the Patriarch, 83; Rabbi Mana, 79; Rabbi Nathan, 114; Rabbi Simlai, 100; Rabbi Simon Ḥasida, 82; Rabbi Yosei ben Ḥalafta, 135; Rabbi Zadok, 93; Rav, 84; Rava, 128; Rav Ami, 20; Rav Huna, 20

Mount Sinai, 100, 110–111, 142, 148

Mount Zion, 148

music, 8, 41, 72, 100

mythology, 20, 51–52, 94

Naḥmanides (Rabbi Moshe ben Naḥman, 1194–1270), 100, 120

nighttime, 18, 36, 64, 82–83, 119, 145; as ideal time for study, 82; as time of darkness, 82

paradox, embrace of, 2–5, 15–16, 27, 32–33, 50, 85–86, 90–91, 98, 119–120, 128–130, 131, 137–138, 141–142, 149, 153, 158

pilgrimage, spiritual growth as modern equivalent of, 1–2, 15, 21, 29, 31, 34, 38, 40, 41–42, 53, 67, 76, 83, 85–86, 90, 100–101, 108, 115, 118–119, 127, 130, 135–136, 148, 150–151, 156, 158

pleasure, 36; in the context of the physical desire, 151, 155; in worship and prayer, 26, 63, 86–87

prayer, 138; as biblically ordained obligation or as commandment, 56–57, 65, 71–72, 75, 97, 157; as bridge to God, 44, 57–58, 77–78; efficacy of, 55, 56, 115; as expression of egotism or smugness, 3, 106; facing east during, 106–107; humility in the context of, 16, 58–59; idiosyncratic nature of, 57–58; language of, 59–61, 87, 144; laws concerning, 16–17, 92; negative response to, 55–56; as part of search for communion with God, 56, 60, 77, 151–152, 155; and silence, 58, 59–60, 65–66, 106; as song or expression of joy, 97–98, 153–154; and widening of the heart, 143–144

raza d'mehemnuta ("the secret of faith"), 137

repentance, 152–153

ritual, vii, ix, 7, 16–18, 25–27, 29–31, 42, 63–67, 69–74, 76, 78–80, 84–86, 91, 93, 96–98, 107, 114–115, 121, 126–128, 130, 139, 140, 142, 150–153, 155–157

Sabbath, 72, 78, 92

selflessness, 66–67, 73–74, 77, 115–116, 132

Shabbat. *See* Sabbath

Shoah, 24, 33; divine non-intervention during, 33; theological implications of, 33

shofar, 108

sorcery, 115–116

submission to God or to God's will or word, 16, 38, 75–77, 81, 87, 89, 90–91, 93–94, 96–98, 100–103, 109–110, 113, 118, 123–125, 139, 141–143, 155, 156

superstition, 26, 98, 115, 142–143
symbolism, 14–15, 19, 25, 35, 39, 46, 53, 64, 67, 100, 105, 106, 137–140, 148, 158

t'fillin, 33
tallit, 118
Ten Commandments, 98, 120
tikkun ha-olam b'malkhut shaddai, 111
Torah, 3, 4, 15, 17, 20, 26, 29, 34, 37, 39, 42, 49, 54, 57, 64–67, 71–72, 76, 82, 86, 89–91, 93, 95–100, 102–104, 110–112, 116, 120, 121, 132, 134–136, 139, 141–149, 151–152, 154–157; of prophets, 148–149; triple aspect of, 154–155
trembling, awe, and dread, x, 14, 56, 65, 76–78, 105–106, 110, 138, 158
truth, vii–viii, x, 2, 4–11, 13–14, 19–21, 23, 24, 32, 33, 37–38, 41, 42, 47–50, 57–60, 63–64, 66, 67, 70, 71, 74, 81, 85–86, 94, 100–102, 105, 106, 110, 114–116, 119–121, 123–125, 129–130, 133, 134, 139–142, 146–147, 150, 155, 159

unhappiness. *See* happiness and unhappiness

variegation, 96–97

worship, 10, 12–13, 16, 17, 19, 26–27, 29, 58, 63–67, 69–87, 92–93, 94, 97–99, 101–103, 105–106, 108, 112–116, 120, 121, 124–126, 128–130, 131–136, 138–139, 142, 144, 145, 147–150, 153–154, 158; as bridge from the world to God, 29, 44, 57–58, 66, 77, 86–87, 120, 123, 128–129, 136, 145, 151; and children, 71–72; Hebrew word for, 64; tainted by arrogance, 56; and urge to self-aggrandize, 65

www.ingramcontent.com/pod-product-compliance
Lightning Source LLC
Chambersburg PA
CBHW032150010526
44111CB00035B/1428